VISITING
SMALL-TOWN
FLORIDA
VOLUME 2

Orange Avenue, "Avenue of the Oaks," in Floral City.

VISITING SMALL-TOWN FLORIDA VOLUME 2

Bruce Hunt

PINEAPPLE PRESS, INC.

Sarasota, Florida

This book is dedicated to my nephew, Ross Hunt, and to my niece, Cameron Logan, both of whom are talented young writers with bright futures, and to the memory of Jack Hardy, the most courageous guy I've ever known.

Copyright © 1999 by Bruce Hunt

Inquiries should be addressed to:
Pineapple Press, Inc.
P.O. Box 3899
Sarasota, Florida 34230-3899

Library of Congress Cataloging in Publication Data
Hunt, Bruce. 1957–
Visiting Small Town Florida Volume 2/ Bruce Hunt. — 1st ed.
p.   cm.
Includes index.
ISBN 1-56164-180-4 (pb : alk. paper)
1. Florida—Guidebooks. 2. Cities and towns—Florida—Guidebooks. I. Title.
F309.3.H86   1999
917.504'63—dc21   98-52986
CIP

First Edition
10 9 8 7 6 5 4 3 2 1

Design by Stacey Arnold

Printed and bound by Edwards Brothers, Lillington, North Carolina

CONTENTS

ACKNOWLEDGMENTS

*T*HE PEOPLE I'VE MET AND CONVERSED WITH in small towns across Florida are as much the authors of this book as I am. Many thanks to Jean Nesbit in Bagdad; Warren Weekes in Milton; Nell King in Two Egg; Debbie Joyner in Quincy; Rita Love and Keith and Lee Hotchkiss in Havana; Nancy Beckham in St. Marks; Maureen Riley in Jasper; Martha and Bill Hargeshiemer in Keaton Beach; Theresa Hamilton and Bill Rataille in Fernandina; Gary Street in Crescent City; Sharon Little and Ginger Blinn in McIntosh; Mary Ann Koslasky, Terrie Adkisson, and everyone at the Citrus County Historical Society in Inverness; Carlotta Yancy in Floral City; Maryann Winters in Ozello; Mary Ann Elliott and Judy Lee in Webster; Rose Harbeck at the Christmas Post Office; Grace Bryant and Walter Roush in Dade City; Alcee Taylor in Cortez; Sarah Bergquist in Estero; and Jane Marquis and Bill Milling in Big Pine Key.

Thanks also to Gerry Hunt, my mom, unpaid P. R. agent, and the biggest promoter of my books; to my aunt, Bonnie Corral, the second biggest promoter of my books; to my ex-wife Barbara Hardy for her continued support and encouragement; to Leslie Kemp Poole and Sharon Kane Monroe, two writer friends who both, long ago, strongly encouraged me to pursue writing; to Loretta Jordan for sharing her insight and her vacation time with me; and to the wonderfully talented folks at Pineapple Press.

INTRODUCTION

O NE OF MY LIFE'S PASSIONS (some would say obsessions) is traveling to places I've never been, places that are remarkably different from where I live.

It seems to me that life at its most basic is really just a collection of experiences. If you always stay in the same place, you won't collect very many. For me, standing at the top of a mountain that I've never been on top of before or taking in a panorama that I've never seen before is an epiphany, a rejuvenation of my soul. It adds to me. It's how I grow.

To gather new experiences and then to share with others the enrichment that I've gained from those experiences is the closest I've been able to come to defining my purpose in life. I guess it's why I write books and take pictures.

Visiting and studying more than seventy small Florida towns over the past three years has been an amazingly enriching experience. *Visiting Small-Town Florida* Volumes 1 and 2 are, on the surface, guides to things to see, things to do, and places to eat. However, between the lines there are other stories being told—not by me but by the people I've met in these vest-pocket communities. Theirs are stories about pursuing happiness, about deciding to improve the quality of their lives and their families' lives, and about following a less conventional path toward achieving those things.

When I first began working on the first volume of *Visiting Small-Town Florida* (Pineapple Press, 1997), I knew there were others who were as enchanted with small towns—and as disenchanted with big cities—as I was. But it was not until after the book came out and I began to do book signings and author appearances that I came to realize how many peo-ple felt the same way I did. That book's success prompted the writing of *Visiting Small-Town Florida* Volume 2. Like Volume 1, this is a travel guidebook, a literal and figurative road map to more of our state's inter-esting, quaint, and sometimes quirky out-of-the-way villages and towns. It is also a window into a sometimes bypassed world.

So, how is it different from the original?

First, *Visiting Small-Town Florida* Volume 2 supplements Volume 1: It covers towns not covered in the original. Beyond that, I have tried to place emphasis on some things that my readers have told me they are most interested in.

Readers told me that knowing the history of a place makes it much more interesting to visit, so I spent a little more time on the historical background of these towns. I've tried to cull out the boring stuff and leave in the interesting, the odd, the trivial, and the humorous stuff. I also wrote a concluding chapter about why I think history is so impor-tant.

Many have told me that they love visiting very tiny, seldom-heard-about places that give them a good excuse to take the long way to wher-ever they're going. So Volume 2 features more very small towns and communities. I have to confess that I have sometimes taken liberty with the term "town." Some of these places are mere crossroads, but I have included them because they are the kinds of places that make the jour-ney more fascinating than the destination. What makes these off-the-beaten-path places interesting is often subtle. While they may not qual-ify as full weekend destinations, these dots on the map are nonetheless well worth plotting your route through.

My readers also told me that they enjoyed hearing about what the people who live and work in these towns have to say, so I've included more conversations I've had with locals. If there is one thing I can label as quintessential small-townness, it is the open friendliness of small-town people.

Much to my gastronomic pleasure, readers also told me that they love eating at good "local cuisine" restaurants, so I've done my best to ferret those out. More than one critic has accused me of writing Eating Your Way Across Small-Town Florida, which I accept with a toothpick-chew-ing grin.

As in Volume 1, I've used a maximum population of ten thousand to define "small town" for the purposes of this book. I know it's an arbitrary number, but I had to choose a cut-off point. The majority of the towns in this volume fit into the fewer-than-three-thousand-people category.

Like the creatures on the isolated Galapagos Islands, many of these places have evolved—even flourished—in their own microcosms apart from the mainstream world. They are eccentric, and they are also fun. I repeatedly found revived Main Streets, exceptional antique shopping, great local food, carefully restored historic structures, and fine examples of century-old Victorian and Florida Cracker homes. The most fun has been meeting and talking to the sometimes-humorous, often-opinionated but always gracious and welcoming people who have chosen to spend their lives in these towns.

The one question I get asked more than any other is which of these towns do I think would be the best to move to. So many of the towns I've visited do look like wonderful places to live—Apalachicola, High Springs, Mount Dora, Havana, Quincy, Fernandina, and Inverness, just to name a few. They all have their allure. I don't think I could pick just one. That's not really the book's purpose, but I know people will use it for that.

Growing interest in small-town life seems to be driven, at least in part, by a distaste for what big cities are now bringing to our doorsteps—crime, traffic, overcrowding. The things that attract us to small towns—neighborliness, safety, a sense of belonging to a community, a sense of living in a place that has its own identity, a little elbow room—have become increasingly scarce in the big cities.

Television and print media have jumped on the bandwagon. Oprah Winfrey did a Small Town Bound show in July 1997. Time ran a cover article in its December 8, 1997, issue called "Why More Americans Are Fleeing to Small Towns." Perhaps the biggest indicator of growing interest in small towns is the expanding popularity of an architectural and town development movement called New Urbanism. The topic has become so hot that I've devoted a short chapter to it at the end of this book.

Small towns are becoming the new frontier. City dwellers, fed up with big city life, are loading up their wagons and heading out of town. Unfortunately, if they look over their shoulders, they might see the city coming right behind them. Florida's ever-exploding population is stretching the boundaries of its large cities. Suburban sprawl is, more frequently than ever, gobbling up these tiny gems of community and robbing them of their uniqueness. Much of Florida's heritage is in these small towns and communities, and I fear that it could one day be obliterated. As Walt Kelly's Pogo was fond of saying: "We have met the enemy, and they is us."

Not to dwell on the negative—there is so much more that is positive about small towns. I have tremendous hope that if enough visitors peer through the window into small-town life and like what they see, maybe they'll take some of the values and some of the sense of community back with them to the city. Like adding water to a dying plant, maybe it will reconstitute their lives with passion.

If you share my vision, then I think you'll enjoy *Visiting Small-Town Florida* Volume 2. So turn the page and follow winding back roads to Florida's tucked-away towns. Tour their historic districts, museums, galleries, antique shops, and great local eateries. Marvel at the intricate architecture of past centuries. Learn about each town's history, and meet some of the unusual and endearing characters who live there today.

NORTH REGION

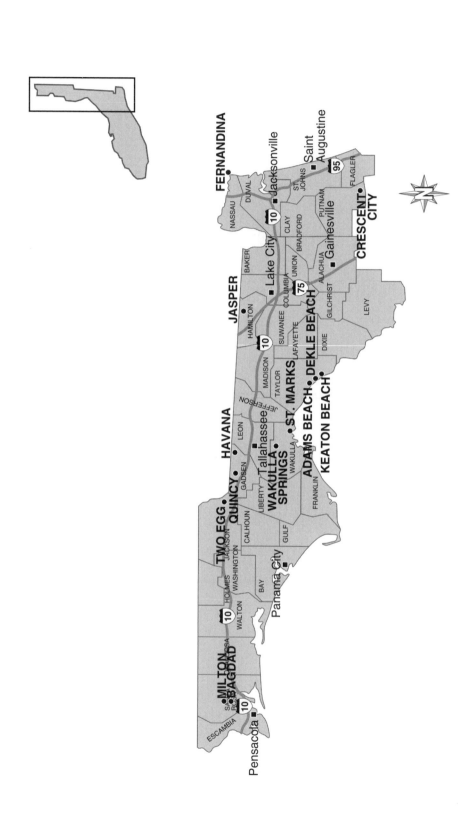

MILTON
AND
BAGDAD

Population: Milton 7,216; Bagdad 350 (estimated)

MILTON AND BAGDAD—the two towns that pine trees built. You can't discuss one without mentioning the other. Separated only by the Pond Creek bayou, their histories and development are inextricably intertwined.

This was logging and sawmill country as early as 1817, when the King of Spain granted land along Pond Creek to Juan de la Rua. De la Rua built and operated a lumber mill there for ten years before becoming discouraged with his inability to keep laborers. In 1828 he sold his property to Joseph Forsyth, who took on partners Ezekiel and Andrew Simpson. They built the dam-driven Arcadia Mill, and a village began to

3

grow around it. The vast forests of this region were thick with valuable long-leaf yellow pine, and the Blackwater River provided a ready highway for floating logs down to Pensacola Bay. Forsyth and the Simpsons prospered, and in 1840 they moved the mill a couple of miles downstream to the juncture of Pond Creek and the Blackwater River. A village grew around it again. This time it took on the name Bagdad—perhaps because, like its Middle-Eastern namesake, it was wedged between two important rivers.

Bagdad grew up on the south side of Pond Creek, and Milton grew up on the north side. About the same time that Joseph Forsyth and the Simpson brothers were getting the Arcadia Mill into full swing, Benjamin and Margaret Jernigan were starting a mill of their own. People began to refer to the area around it as Jernigan's Landing and also as Scratch Ankle—presumably because of the dense briars that grew along the banks of the Blackwater River. Neither of those names stuck, but a more definitive one, Milltown, did, and it eventually evolved into Milton, which was incorporated in 1844.

More sawmills opened over the next few decades. By the turn of the century, Milton and Bagdad had become the most industrialized towns in Florida. The lumber barons thought the bounty was endless, but they were short-sighted. The Crash of 1929 hit both towns hard. Plus, the once-plentiful pine forests had become depleted. The last of the mills, the Bagdad Land & Lumber Company, closed in 1939.

Santa Rosa County Road 191 becomes Forsyth Street for a brief dozen or so blocks as it passes through Bagdad. About three-quarters of the way through town, on the west side of Forsyth Street, I pull into the Old Mill House Gallery. Owner Jean Nesbit moved to Bagdad in 1973. She and her husband bought the circa-1880, wood-frame, two-family house in 1988. Slowly but surely they restored it and then opened the Gallery to display and sell handwoven rugs and wall hangings, jewelry, sketches, paintings, wood sculpture, and pottery. When I walk in, my first thought is that she should add "and Museum" to the end of the name.

"This was a duplex," Jean recounts, "built by the Simpson Sawmill Company about a hundred and twenty years ago. When we bought it, the floor hung four inches below the baseboards. Termites had eaten it

Bagdad Village Preservation Association Museum, located in the building that was Bagdad's first African-American church.

up. We have replaced eight-inch sills from the back corner of the house, out to and across the front, and down the other side. We've replaced nearly the whole front. We are trying to retain the old windows. You can see these old glass panes are the kind with waves and bubbles in them. Unfortunately, the termites got into the frames."

About the same time they bought the house, the Nesbits started an unusual business (for Florida)—raising sheep. "I had been given an old table loom, so I took weaving lessons," Jean explains. "One day the county agriculture agent suggested to my husband and me, 'What you really should do is start from the very basics and work up.' So we acquired a sheep, and one became seven, which became twelve, which became a hundred. It's very labor intensive. We did it for about ten years, and we truly did enjoy it, but now that we're getting closer to retirement age, we are ready to move on to something else. We had annual shearings [for both their own sheep and those they had sold to others] that would last two days. It was quite a sight. Some of the people who only owned

*The 1913/1914 Exchange Hotel in Milton is now
the First Judicial State Attorney's office.*

one or two would show up with their sheep on a leash with a dog collar. Two years ago we had one hundred sheep and twenty-five angora goats. Now we have just two sheep—two chubby, healthy, happy sheep."

Jean has done it all: shearing, cleaning the fiber, spinning, weaving. "I guess I'm a throwback from somewhere in the past, but I really enjoy it," she says. "It's therapeutic. My husband says 'It's much cheaper than a psychiatrist.' I ask him, 'How would you know this?'" In one room she has a large LeClerc loom (modern, not antique). Threads from spools of spun wool are vectored through the loom's teeth, and an ornately patterned rug spills out the other side. Jean also teaches spinning and weaving—to those who have the patience for it—on a one-on-one basis.

As I mentioned, the gallery looks more like a museum. In addition to the weavings, pieces that Jean has for sale range from wood carvings (there's a wooden rocking chair with Mom and Pop figures carved into the back posts), to some charming linocut prints of dogs, to pottery with lifelike lizards and frogs on them, to intricately woven pine needle baskets, to marvelously detailed pen-and-ink prints and acrylic paintings.

Bagdad seems like the perfect setting for Jean's gallery. She tells me, "When people come to Bagdad to visit, they are entranced. It's like another world, with its big trees filled with Spanish moss and beautiful old homes, like the Thompson House."

The Thompson House, across the street from Old Mill House Gallery, predates the Civil War. Mill owner Benjamin Thompson built the two-story antebellum mansion, with its double front porches and twelve white columns. During the Civil War, invading Union troops commandeered the house. (By then most of the townspeople had fled.) Before moving on, they left a message, scrawled in charcoal across a wall in the parlor, that is still there today: "Mr. Thompson, Spurling's First Cavalry camped in your house on the 26th of October, 1864." Originally the house overlooked the Blackwater River, a few blocks to the east, but in 1912 the owners must have wanted a change of scenery. They jacked the house up onto log rollers, turned it around 180 degrees, and pulled it by mule to its present location. The D'Asaro family, the house's current owners, built removable paneling in the parlor to preserve the historic scribblings.

"Bagdad is small enough that everybody pretty much knows everybody else—makes for a great gossip mill," according to Jean. "It is inhabited mostly by families who have lived here for generations. We have all ages. These are very kind, very friendly people. They have genuine concern for you, your family, your kids. We have a grandchild who will be starting this fall at Bagdad Elementary. Hopefully, the teachers won't remember the antics of his elders."

Across the road and around the corner on Thompson Street, I stop to take a picture of the old Bagdad post office, a tiny wooden building with only one window. It belongs to the Bagdad Village Preservation Association. Right now it is boarded up, but it looks ripe for restoration. The building went into service in 1913 and closed in 1986. Four blocks south and a block west of Forsyth Street, at the corner of Bushnell and Church Streets, is the Bagdad Village Preservation Association's Museum in a building that was once Bagdad's first African-American church.

Across Pond Creek Bridge, Milton has grown into a sizable town, with a population of over seven thousand. The downtown district has had some renovation, particularly on Caroline Street (Highway 90) and Willing Street, which parallels the Blackwater River. Downtown reminds me of a miniature Savannah or New Orleans French Quarter. A new Riverwalk Park—with pink-blossoming crepe myrtle trees, brick walkways, wrought-iron-and-wood park benches, gas lamp–style street lights, and a dock—lines the waterfront behind Willing Street.

Devastating fires swept through the downtown in 1909 and again in 1911, leveling much of the district. But this was boom-time in Milton, and the town was rebuilt bigger and better than before. Two notable brick buildings, the three-story Imogene Theater on Caroline Street between Elmira and Willing Streets and the Exchange Hotel at the corner of Caroline and Elmira Streets, were part of Milton's rebirth from the ashes.

Architect Walker Willis designed the theater. It was originally called the Milton Opera House when it opened in 1912. When the Gootch family bought it in 1920, they renamed it after their eleven-year-old daughter, Imogene. A post office and a store shared the first floor. The upstairs theater ran vaudeville shows and silent movies and later "talkies" until it closed in 1946. The Santa Rosa Historical Society restored it in 1987. Its offices, along with the Milton Opera House Museum of Local History, now occupy a portion of the building.

Charles Sudmall, who operated the local telephone exchange, was so impressed with the Milton Opera House that he hired the same contractor, S. F. Fulguhm Company from Pensacola, to build the Exchange Hotel in 1913. Sudmall insisted that the hotel architecturally match the Opera House. The hotel closed around 1946, but it was restored in 1984 and is now the First Judicial Circuit State Attorney's office.

From downtown, I follow Caroline Street (Highway 90) west, past Pensacola Junior College, then turn north on Anna Simpson Road, and west again on Mill Pond Road, which dead ends at a trail head for the Arcadia Mill Archeological Site. On the left, a driveway leads up to the Arcadia Mill Site Museum.

Warren Weekes, the museum's curator, tells me about Arcadia in the 1840s. "Back then, you were not allowed to acquire property and then turn right around to resell it. When Juan de la Rua got this property from the King of Spain, he had to keep it, improve it, and work it for a minimum of seven years. He paid the King of Spain one shipload of square lumber, per year, in taxes. When de la Rua sold the property to John Forsyth for four hundred dollars, he was glad to get rid of it. De la Rua wasn't much for running the mill. He was more interested in politics—went on later to become mayor of Pensacola. The Arcadia Mill ran off of two big water wheels driven by Pond Creek. The mill made square lumber with straight saws—the round saw wasn't invented until after 1840. They would cut the long-leaf yellow pine lengthwise, flip it on its side, then cut it again, so that it came out square."

Forsyth moved the mill in 1840 when he acquired a steam engine to replace the water wheels. The engine allowed him to set up the mill at the mouth of the river, which facilitated transporting the lumber.

The Arcadia Mill Site Museum displays artifacts excavated from the Arcadia site by the University of West Florida's Archaeology Department, as well as a collection of old photographs from the mill's era.

I follow the trail into the woods, over a rise and down into a ravine, where it crosses a swinging wooden bridge spanning Pond Creek. This was the site of the Arcadia Mill dam and water wheels. Beneath the clear water of Pond Creek, I can still see the remains of a rock wall—a part of what was once the foundation of the dam—built into the bank of the creek.

Back on County Road 191, another restored Milton historical structure, the 1909 Milton Railroad Depot, sits next to still-operating railroad tracks just across the Pond Creek Bridge. Although trains still run on these tracks, they no longer stop here. The original depot, built in 1882, burned in 1907. The 1909 depot was part of the Louisville and Nashville Railroad system. When passenger trains were discontinued in 1973, the depot closed and fell quickly into disrepair. The following year, the Santa Rosa Historical Society was formed to try to save it, which they did. The depot reopened on July 4, 1976. It now houses the West Florida Railroad Museum.

The depot's front office is a shop that sells everything for the model train afficionado—tracks, trains, scenery, scale buildings and figures, and books. After browsing the shelves and glass cases filled with HO and other scale model trains, I walk around the side to the museum. Outside, loudspeakers that monitor the railroad radio channel add to the ambiance. Inside the museum, what were once passenger-waiting and cargo-loading areas now display different types of track; old conductor's uniforms, including hats from as far back as 1910; and old railroad track-laying tools, like a Buda-Clark track liner tool from 1920. There is also a collection of restored railway switches, crossing lights, and signals. One of the crossing signals is a 1917 Model 2A semaphore signal that was used by the North Pacific Railway on Stampede Pass in the Cascade Mountain Range in Washington state. They even have an old hand-and-foot-propelled velocipede railbike.

The ticket booth and the waiting room have been restored to their early twentieth-century appearance. Outside there are two restored railroad cars. One contains offices; the other is a dining car, complete with running ceiling fans and dining tables with full place settings—which reminds me that it's dinner time.

An acquaintance of Jean Nesbit whom I met in the Old Mill House

The 1909 Milton Railroad Depot was restored by the Santa Rosa Historical Society and reopened on July 4, 1976.

Gallery has recommended the Cutting Board Restaurant in Milton—and a good recommendation it is. Owners Steve and Laura House bought the 1928 tongue-and-groove-board, wood-frame house and converted it into a restaurant in 1997. Their specialty is fresh-from-local-waters seafood—crawfish, shrimp, blue crab claws, oysters, mullet, and snapper—but they also serve steaks and chicken. I start with a big bowl of their "Big South" gumbo, which would receive raves at any French Quarter restaurant. It is thick with fish, crab, and shrimp and is very spicy. Then I have a heaping plate of steamed blue crab claws, already shelled and dusted with unidentified Cajun seasonings: a filling ending to a full day.

DIRECTIONS: Take Santa Rosa County Road 191 north from Interstate 10.

DON'T MISS: Old Mill House Gallery

ADDRESSES AND EVENTS: See page 148

TWO EGG

Population: 28

ONE HALF BLOCK from the junction of Jackson County Road 69 and County Road 69A (better known locally as Wintergreen Road), the Lawrence Grocery Store sits at the center of all activity in Two Egg, Florida. Actually, it's the only activity in Two Egg. At one time, the Pittman Store across the street competed with it, but it's been closed now since Mr. Pittman retired in 1984.

Nell Lawrence King has owned the Lawrence Grocery since 1988. It has been in her family for the better part of four decades. Her father, her uncle, and her brothers have all owned it at one time or another. When I walk through the screen door, Nell smiles and welcomes me with a

"Howdy." I don't want her to think I'm with the IRS or anything, so I explain that I'm gathering research for my book on small towns.

"I've lived within a couple miles from here all my life," Nell tells me. "This is the entire town of Two Egg. Let me count up for a second and I'll tell you what the population is." For about five seconds, Nell mentally ticks off in her head who has had babies lately. "Should be twenty-eight right now. Yeah, we may be a small town, but people do know we're here. The Florida Department of Transportation folks over in Tallahassee tell us that the 'Two Egg' road sign out on County Road 69 is the most stolen road sign in the whole state."

"You already know what my first question is going to be, don't you?" I ask Nell.

"Yep," she responds. "How did it get to be named Two Egg? It is Two Egg, by the way, not Two Eggs. It was originally named Allison. Back in the 1890s, a salesman who stopped here frequently on his route started calling it Two Egg. Every time he would come into the store, he would see the little children of a local farm-working family—the Williamses—bringing in eggs to trade for sodas or candy. It was a large family. In lieu of an allowance, each had a chicken to care for—and they could use the eggs from their chickens to barter at the store. The smaller children could just manage one egg in each hand, hence the name Two Egg. Mr. Will Williams comes in here to sit and visit regularly. He says it was his grandfather's children—Will's aunts and uncles—who traded eggs at the store back then. Will tells me that his grandfather had fifty-seven children by three wives."

Customers are coming and going while we talk. Nell knows each of them on a first-name basis. I notice that with some customers there is no exchange of money, and I ask Nell why.

"Well, it's something you don't see hardly anymore, but we still run an account for our regular customers. In addition to groceries, we sell gas, oil, and batteries, hardware, nuts, and bolts. This is peanut farming territory, so we get a lot of business from the farmers. My local customers come from within about a ten-mile radius of here. Oftentimes they'll sit for a while and have coffee and talk. Plus, I get tourists in here every day. In the summer, the tour buses stop here. I sell a lot of Two Egg caps and T-shirts."

Nell Lawrence King's Lawrence Grocery Store in Two Egg (population 28).

When I ask Nell if she's ever had anyone famous stop in, she pulls a thick guest book out from under the counter and goes directly to a page from September 1992. She points to Faye Dunaway's signature. "You know, she was raised in Bascom, about six miles north of here," Nell explains. "She went to school with my husband. When she came in to the store in 1992, she stayed for a good thirty minutes and talked to all the customers who came in. She was interested to know if any of them had known her dad."

Nell's father, Mr. Lawrence, walks in and pulls up a chair. I ask him about the history of the store, and he tells me that Mathis Pittman built the store and owned it for quite some time before selling it to the Powell family. Mr. Lawrence bought it from Johnny Powell in the mid-1960s.

Nell continues her family's tradition and points out that she has now owned the store longer than any of the other Lawrences. Six days a week she opens at 6:30 A.M. and closes at 7:00 in the evening, sometimes later if folks are chatting.

DIRECTIONS: Take Jackson County Road 69 north from Interstate 10 (east of Marianna) to County Road 69A.

DON'T MISS: Two Egg! Don't blink or you will.

ADDRESSES AND EVENTS: See page 149

QUINCY

Population: 7,444

*A*PPROACHING QUINCY FROM THE EAST ON HIGHWAY 12, I pass by a stand of oaks densely spider-webbed with kudzu. It's a reminder that the topography at this northern end of the state blends seamlessly with southern Alabama and southern Georgia. The town of Quincy does the same thing. It's the Gadsden County seat, and like so many small towns in the heart of the South, it has a stately dome-topped courthouse with four massive white columns in the middle of the town square. A Civil War monument on the south side of the courthouse reads, "Sacred to the memory of the Confederate soldiers from Gadsden County, Florida, who died in the defense of their country."

I'm arriving at lunch time. I've read good things about the Gadsden Carriage House Restaurant, located in a cellar beneath the old May Tobacco Company Building, one half block east of the town square. Built in 1906, the building was originally a farm equipment and grain company. The May Tobacco Company bought it in 1920. In 1988 native Hollander Dutch Swart and his wife Sofia purchased the building and opened their restaurant downstairs. Before coming to Quincy, Dutch was a chef at Brennan's in New Orleans and also worked for famous chef Paul Prudhomme. The evening menu features European entrees and soups alongside some Creole specialties.

From the sidewalk on Washington Street, I pass through a wrought iron gate, into a French Quarter–style courtyard, and down a winding brick stairway to enter the Carriage House. They have set up a grand Southern country lunch buffet. For a ridiculously low $4.99, I stack my plate with the same kind of Southern dishes my grandmother used to prepare: fried chicken, beef stew, roast pork (so tender it falls apart when I pick it up) and gravy, macaroni and cheese, collard greens, lima beans cooked with ham hocks, okra and tomato, white acre beans (like tiny, sweet black-eyed peas), candied yams, and squash.

After that delicious feast, I decide that a walk is a good idea. Debbie Joyner of the Quincy Chamber of Commerce has given me a pamphlet guide to the historic downtown buildings and the antebellum and post–Civil War homes in the surrounding neighborhood. It lists more than fifty structures—all worth seeing. A few among those that I find most interesting architecturally are the Queen Anne–Victorian McFarlin House on East King Street, built by tobacco planter John McFarlin in 1895 and now a bed-and-breakfast; the Allison House (also a bed-and-breakfast) on North Madison Street, built in 1843 by General A. K. Allison, who would serve as governor of Florida in 1865; the 1910 Bell & Bates Hardware building on North Madison Street (the north side of the town square); the 1949 Leaf Theatre building on East Washington Street (in the same block as the May Tobacco Company building/Carriage House Restaurant); the red-brick Quincy Academy building on North Adams Street, built in 1851; and the Quincy Mercantile building/Quincy State Bank, built in 1893, on the northeast corner of the town square at Washington and Madison.

The MacFarlin House Bed & Breakfast in
Quincy was built by tobacco farmer John
MacFarlin in 1895.

1906 Tobacco Company building in Quincy. The
Carriage House Restaurant is in the basement.

Restored 1851 Quincy Academy building.

There is an interesting historical side note that connects Quincy with the Coca-Cola Company. In the early 1900s, patrons of the Quincy State Bank (Florida's first chartered state bank) were told that purchasing stock in a fledgling drink company might prove to be a good investment. Lots of Quincyites took that advice and became wealthy. For many years, residents in Quincy held more than half of Coca-Cola's outstanding shares. Today they are still thought to own as much as ten percent of Coca-Cola's stock.

DIRECTIONS: Take Highway 267 exit north from I-10.

DON'T MISS: Gadsden Carriage House Restaurant

ADDRESSES AND EVENTS: See page 149

HAVANA

Population: 1,654

*H*EADING NORTH OUT OF TALLAHASSEE, the scenery on U. S. Highway 27 begins to look less like Florida and more like Georgia— rolling hills and red clay, more pine trees than palm trees. This was part of my trade route from Tampa to Auburn, Alabama, when I attended Auburn University in the mid- and late 1970s. About fifteen miles north of the Capitol, Highway 27 passes through Havana. I recall it as a sedate, somewhat boarded-up little town whose tobacco farming–based economy had dried up ten years before. My only specific recollection of Havana is that it's where I once received a speeding ticket at 1:00 A.M.

What a difference two decades makes! Havana is a town reborn. The downtown district has been richly restored. Antique shops, art galleries, and quaint cafes have turned it into a destination for browsers from all over the South.

My first stop is an old-fashioned country store called the Little River General Store. It's a half block north of Seventh Avenue on Main Street (Highway 27). In keeping with the true definition of a general store, they have a little bit of everything in here: food (lots of sauces and spices), an entire counter full of candy, dry goods, soaps, cookware, kerosene lamps, furniture, rugs, gardening tools, and kitchen utensils. The product packaging and the brands remind me of those from a bygone era. The store's brick walls, wood plank floors, and wood tables and display counters add to the old-fashioned atmosphere.

Rita Love is the proprietor, and she tells me that she moved up to the Havana/Tallahassee area from the central part of the state in 1974. "I just love it up here in north Florida—sometimes we call it south Georgia," she smiles. "The ruralness of it, the peacefulness. My husband, Jim, and I live about two miles from the store, and we don't have to drive through a single traffic light to get here. The pace is more easygoing; life is a little simpler—like the good old days. People still grow their own gardens, put stuff up in cans and jars. That's why I have this store. It reminds me—and I hope it reminds the people who come in—of a simpler time."

I ask Rita about the unusual brands and products, and she responds, "We do have some terrific brands. One of my favorites is the Watkins line. Mr. Watkins started his business in 1868, selling out of his horse and buggy both to general stores and to homes, door-to-door. He was famous for his vanilla extract. Today they sell very high-quality spices and food products—like this 'sneezeless' pepper, which they import from Europe."

All manner of household supplies and hardware stack the shelves behind the counter. "We have soap, salves, and balms," she points out. "In the candy case we've got black licorice, jaw breakers, bubble gum cigars. We even have Necco wafers and Moon pies. In the back, we just put in an old horizontal Coca-Cola cooler box. It's stocked with Cokes, root beer, and orange sodas."

In the middle of our conversation, my tape recorder batteries go dead. "What's it take," Rita asks, "two double As?" Of course, she has them on the shelf right behind her. "You should meet Keith Henderson and Lee Hotchkiss, around the corner at H & H Antiques. They bought and restored this entire block of old brick buildings in the early 1980s and kick-started the whole rejuvenation of Havana." I make a note to look up Keith and Lee. "Havana's a great town to live in. Southern hospitality abounds. We have wonderful neighbors. We wouldn't want to live anywhere else."

On my way out I notice a T-shirt hanging on the wall that has a phonetic spelling and definition of Havana printed on the front: "Ha-van-a (hey-van-a). n. 1. a picturesque village in North Florida; pop. 1,893. 2. a cigar. 3. the art and antique capital of the Western Hemisphere. 4. the real South. syn.—Paradise on Earth."

On Rita's advice, I walk down to H & H Antiques. H & H occupies the bottom floor of a restored 1908 two-story brick building on the northwest corner of Seventh Avenue and Main Street (Highway 27). Jasmine ivy grows across the front entrance, up to the second floor, and then around the corner. An old stained-glass window adjacent to the front door depicts a barmaid serving Molly Malone beer. If Sherlock Holmes were to walk out the door, it would complete my impression of this as an old English pub.

Inside, the store is filled with antique furniture—dressers, beds, china cabinets, even a couple of grandfather clocks. One entire room is dedicated to antique china. In the corner room, the jasmine vine has grown inside through a gap in a window. It crawls up across the ceiling and down one wall.

Lee Hotchkiss is unloading a box of china tea cups and saucers when I introduce myself.

"Keith [her husband] and I ran our antique shop in Tallahassee for five years," she begins, "before we moved here in 1982. We had always loved the look of Havana. We originally were just interested in the one corner building, but the owners wanted to sell the whole block and made us such an attractive offer that we bought it all. That was in 1981. We talked to all our antique-business friends in Tallahassee about the idea of an antique district in downtown Havana. They loved it, and four of them decided to move their stores here and rent space in the block!

The McLauchlin House, a circa-1840s "dogwalk-style" farmhouse, was restored and relocated from Decatur County, Georgia, to Havana. It's now an antiques shop.

Rita Love's old-fashioned Little River General Store in Havana.

We spent that entire summer and fall renovating. We sandblasted six coats of this awful green paint off the walls. We pulled out the drop ceiling, pulled out all the drywall so that the brick interior walls would show. We put in the wood floors, built cabinets and shelves. It was a chore, and we did it all ourselves. The first weekend we opened up, there were five shops in the block. It was a hit from day one!"

Lee offers me hot tea, and we sit at an antique overstuffed sofa and coffee table. Keith Henderson joins us, and I ask about the history of this building. "The building was built in 1908, two years after the town of Havana was incorporated," Keith tells me.

"This corner building, the one we're in," Lee explains, "was a pharmacy for many years. The rest of the block was a hardware store and department store."

I had read that Lee and Keith also owned the McLauchlin House, a large restored "dogwalk floor plan" farmhouse, one block west of here. It has a wide wraparound covered porch with ornate Victorian gingerbread trim. They rent the interior space out to several different antique shop owners. When I ask about the house, a smile forms on Keith's face. "That's an interesting story," he says. "The McLauchlin House was built in the 1840s. It was on a farm about twenty miles north of here in Decatur County, Georgia. One of the local residents who lives here in Havana, Nellie McLauchlin Cantey, was born in the house in 1899. She also married her husband, Joe Cantey, in the house in 1919. When Nellie's brother passed away, the family considered selling the farm. Lee and I went up there to buy some of the furniture, and we just fell in love with the house. We talked to them about buying it, along with some of the acreage. It turns out that the family really wanted to keep the property, but no one was going to live in the house. Then Nellie came up with a wonderful plan. She offered to give us the house by itself for free with two conditions: one, that we pay the expense to move the house and two, that we move it to Havana, where she could be near it. Needless to say, we accepted her offer. The house movers had to cut it into three sections to transport it."

"When I first started cleaning out the closets, I found a contractor's lumber bill for building materials to add the wraparound porch. It was dated 1899. Cypress shake roof, all the gingerbread trim, columns, floor

The Cannery in Havana, remodeled into a restaurant and shops complex, once housed the Havana Canning Company, which supplied canned fruits and vegetables to U.S. troops during World War II.

and ceiling lumber for one hundred and forty-two feet of porch—the total bill was only seventy-two dollars! Not long after we finished fixing it up, Nellie and Joe, who are still living, by the way, celebrated their seventy-fifth wedding anniversary in the house."

Lee and Keith tell me that they spend more time these days in the real estate business than in the antique business. You wouldn't think that by wandering through their store, though. They've diversified H & H Antiques. One room has been turned into a women's clothes boutique. They also just began carrying a line of new sofas.

"The downtown district has grown continuously since the mid-1980s," Lee says. "At first we thought that we would only draw customers from Tallahassee, but people come here every week from all over Florida and Georgia. Most all the shops and cafes in Havana are open Wednesday through Sunday. We all take off Monday and Tuesday—we call it the 'Havana weekend'."

All the merchants in Havana are within easy walking distance of one

The 1828 Nicholson Farmhouse Restaurant near Havana was once
the home of north Florida pioneer, Dr. Malcolm Nicholson.

another. One block east of Main Street (Highway 27), I walk into the Florida Art Center and Gallery on First Street. Watercolor artist (and former Tallahassee television newscaster) Lee Mainella operates the spacious gallery and artists' workshop. In addition to his own work, the works of other artists from around north Florida and south Georgia are on display—watercolors, oils, and some exceptional marble sculpture.

Next door to the Art Center, I duck into Dolly's Expresso Cafe for a fresh-baked cranberry muffin and a coffee. They have an enticing selection of sweets, including something I've never seen before—key lime fudge.

Antique stores are Havana's main draw, and there are plenty of those. Some specialize in certain types of items. A small place in the middle of the block on First Street NW called Antiques and Accents features mahogany furniture from the eighteenth and nineteenth centuries. Most of the pieces are large, like a tall, early 1800s, four-poster "plantation bed" that the owner tells me she found up in Bruton, Alabama.

Across Main Street, on East Seventh Avenue, it's the aroma that invites me into an interesting shop named Kudzu Plantation. Dried flowers, the specialty, fill one whole wall. Unusual odds and ends, like vintage luggage and old wicker furniture, make up the rest of their inventory. They have a display case filled with old (antique?) fishing lures, bobbers, weights, and knives. Old rods and reels hang in a rack nearby. The Happy Hippo, one half block east, occupies the enclosed front porch of Mary Ann Dziezyc's home. She specializes in antique jewelry, china, crystal, ceramic figures, and, of course, lots of hippopotamus items!

For lunch, I cross back over to First Street NW to the Twin Willow Cafe. All the tables in their French Quarter–style courtyard are occupied, so I take a seat inside, where full-size willow trees painted on the walls make me feel I'm outside. Their chalkboard menu changes daily. Among today's choices are chili-cheese quiche and a Southern vegetable plate. I opt for their Modesto salad, and it is a delicious choice: mandarin orange slices, purple onion, raisins, dry-roasted peanuts, toasted sesame seeds, and vermouth-curry dressing mixed in with leafy organic greens.

After lunch, I continue my walking tour. Over on Second Street NW, a building marked "1931" houses the Planter's Exchange. The sign says "Hardware," but there's a lot more than that. In addition to a full array of outdoor and gardening supplies, they have interesting outdoor furniture, like park benches and double rockers. They also have mailboxes, bird baths, garden statues, and fountains, but I'm most intrigued by their collection of patina-finished copper weather vanes. (Patina is that green coating that forms naturally on copper after it's been outdoors.)

Back on the other side of Main Street on East Eighth Avenue is a renovated, red-brick vegetable canning warehouse. The Cannery is now home to two restaurants, more than a dozen shops, and hundreds of individual booths. It's a maze—actually several warehouse buildings connected to one another. Back in the early 1940s, Mrs. Eulia Stephens decided to expand her home canning business into a full-fledged fruit and vegetable packing plant. Vegetable growing was big business around Havana in those days. With the start of World War II and the demand for long–shelf life food to feed the troops, the Havana Canning Company was canning nearly seven million pounds of fruit and vegetables a year. When the canning business faded in the early 1960s, Cal Albritton bought the facility to pack his Tupelo honey. Three decades later, it was purchased again and remodeled into the restaurant-and-antique-shops complex that I've become lost in this afternoon. Just when I think I've browsed through the entire place, I find another door that leads me into yet another room—even larger than the previous one—filled with shops. The front section contains the restaurants and some of the larger boutiques. Small booths, each one with something different to offer, fill the back section. Most of them sell antiques, collectibles, or memorabilia. Some sell artwork. One booth that I found particularly interesting was Sherrill McNeece's Photographic Art booth. She has an exceptional eye, and her photographs are beautiful. What makes them very unusual is that she hand-tints them using transparent oil paints.

Havana has done a remarkable job of creating something new out of the remains of its old. The town was originally incorporated in 1906 and was named in honor of the Cuban tobacco that had been widely cultivated in this area for the previous three quarters of a century. In later years, tobacco farmers in Havana developed a specialization in growing "shade tobacco," the leaves of which cigar makers use as the outer wrapper of the cigar. They called it shade tobacco because they grew it under cheese-cloth tarps that let just the right amount of light through in order to grow perfect leaves. The harvested leaves were then carefully dried over charcoal pit fires. The entire operation was a delicate process. In the mid-1960s, under a United States Government foreign goodwill program, the north Florida shade tobacco growers' special farming and harvesting techniques were taught to several South American countries. Within just a couple of years, these countries were producing shade tobacco at a significantly lower cost, and the growing industry around Havana (and consequently the town itself) died. It would be almost two more decades before Keith Henderson and Lee Hotchkiss would come along and begin CPR on its downtown district.

By late afternoon, I have wandered up and down all of the streets and through most of the shops. I am anxiously anticipating dinner this evening at the Nicholson Farmhouse Restaurant, about three miles east of Havana on State Road 12—so anxiously, in fact, that I show up an hour early for my 7:00 P.M. reservation. No problem. They gladly seat me right away.

Scottish immigrant Dr. Malcolm Nicholson built the seven-room plantation farmhouse sometime around 1828. It is among the oldest in Gadsden County. He constructed it using lumber from pine trees on his own property. Hand-formed bricks were stacked inside its wood-frame walls for added insulation. Nicholson was a prominent physician and a planter and was active in the early development of the north-central region of Florida. He was on the original committee that chose Tallahassee as Florida's state capital in 1824.

The farm remained in the Nicholson family until 1971, when it was sold to the Eubanks family, who did a lot of restoration work on the house. Paul Nicholson, great-great-grandson of Dr. Malcolm Nicholson, and his wife, Ann, bought the house back in 1987, along with the sur-rounding fifty acres, and opened the restaurant. The farmhouse, the adjacent smoke house, and a barn are original buildings. Paul and Ann relocated several more vintage buildings to the property: the Littman farmhouse, built in 1890, from a couple of miles down State Road 12; the Shady Rest Tourist Camp building (it looks like an old Wild West hotel), built in 1927, also from just down the road; and the Overstreet, Florida, Post Office/Patrick's General Store. Overstreet is near the coast about halfway between Apalachicola and Panama City. Thomas Patrick built the structure in 1916, and members of the Patrick family operat-ed it continuously until 1991. Paul and Ann purchased it and moved it to the Nicholson farm in 1995.

Cars parked out in front of the main farmhouse are my only clue that I haven't traveled backwards in a time machine. A dirt road leads me from the gate off State Road 12 across the Nicholson property, where a white gazebo sits by itself in the middle of the pasture. The farm's half dozen structures form what looks like a tiny, sleepy, country communi-ty from before the turn of the century. When I roll past the barn, two mules stick their heads out and watch me go by. (I later find out their names are Kate and Emma.) As I walk through the picket fence gate, one of the Nicholson family dogs—a tail-wagging yellow Lab—ambles up to greet me. Inside, the farmhouse decor includes a mixture of wood-frame and brick walls with solid pine beams across the ceiling. It feels like a home. After all, that's what it was for more than a century.

Steaks are the Nicholson Farmhouse specialty. They cut and age their own beef. I order the tenderloin fillet. Although I don't ordinarily assassinate a good steak with steak sauce, I do sample some of the Nicholson Farmhouse's own. It's made with Vidalia onions, vinegar, mustard, tomatoes, and something else (unidentified) that gives it a tangy, sweet flavor. My entrée comes with a baked stuffed potato, whipped (with cheese and sour cream) to a soufflé consistency; a salad with whole pickled okra; fresh green beans; and hot-out-of-the-oven rolls—all of which is superb, as is my peanut butter pie dessert.

After dinner, I walk through the Nicholson-Freeman Cemetery on the east side of the property. Dr. Malcolm Nicholson shares a headstone with his wife, Mary. The epitaph on one side reads, "Called the Father of Medicine in Florida."

On my way back to Havana, the sun is setting behind me, and I'm enjoying the scenery as the sun lights up all the color in the trees and the rolling hills. Rita Love is right: this is a peaceful, easygoing place. I roll down my window to let the country air blow through. When I glance at my speedometer, I realize that I'm driving fifteen miles per hour under the speed limit.

DIRECTIONS: Travel twelve miles north of Tallahassee on Highway 27.

DON'T MISS: Nicholson Farmhouse Restaurant, Little River General Store & Trading Company

ADDRESSES AND EVENTS: See page 149

WAKULLA SPRINGS

Population: 500 (estimated)

"CENTURIES OF PASSION PENT UP IN HIS SAVAGE HEART!" is the tag line on the movie posters for Universal Studio's 1954 sci-fi/horror classic *The Creature from the Black Lagoon*. Archaeologists (played by Richard Carlson and Julie Adams) discover the prehistoric gill-man/monster (Ben Chapman) while on expedition deep in the Amazon. The film was a special effects/technological marvel in its day—filmed in 3-D, mostly underwater. Universal chose Wakulla Springs, fifteen miles south of Tallahassee, for the filming location because of its exceptionally clear waters.

Wakulla Springs is the largest and deepest spring in the world. Its waters are so clear that details at the bottom—185 feet deep—are easily discernible from the surface. It actually has been the site of numerous archaeological excavations. In 1935, divers discovered a complete mastodon skeleton at the bottom of the spring. The mastodon now stands, reconstructed, in the Museum of Florida History in the R. A. Gray Building at the Capitol in Tallahassee.

The springs had its own recently living, prehistoric creature, too—although by all accounts it was not a malevolent one. Old Joe was a 650-pound, 11-foot-2-inch alligator that had been seen at the springs since the 1920s. Although he had never shown aggressive behavior, an unknown assailant shot and killed Old Joe in August 1966. Old Joe was estimated to be 200 years old. Carl Buchheister, then president of the Audubon Society, offered a $5000 reward for information leading to the arrest of the gunman, but no one was ever charged with killing Old Joe.

All manner of wildlife thrives in the park. Deer, raccoons, and even a few bears live here in addition to alligators. Bird watchers can spot a variety of winged creatures—anhingas, purple gallinules, herons, egrets, ospreys, and long-billed limpkins (called "crying birds" because of their shrieking, almost humanlike cry).

When I pass through the entrance gate to the Edward Ball Wakulla Springs State Park, the park ranger warns me to be cautious if I hike the trail down to the Sally Ward Spring. "Where you see the red ribbons," she tells me, "that marks the area where one of our momma gators is keeping close watch over her new brood of babies. Needless to say, she's being very protective." I assure the park ranger that I won't go anywhere near the Sally Ward Spring and that I'm actually here to see the lodge.

Edward Ball was the brother-in-law of Alfred I. DuPont. He was also the executor and trustee of DuPont's sizable estate and trust. Ball built a banking, telephone, railroad, and paper-and-box manufacturing empire out of the DuPont trust. Dupont's estate was worth an estimated thirty-three million dollars in 1935 when he died. Ball had grown that into more than two billion dollars by the time he passed away in 1981 at age 93.

One of Edward Ball's proudest achievements was the construction of the Wakulla Springs Lodge in 1937. The twenty-seven-room lodge is essentially the same today as it was in the 1930s. Ball insisted that it

The 185-foot-deep Wakulla Springs, where 1954 sci-fi/horror classic The Creature from the Black Lagoon *and numerous* Tarzan *features were filmed.*

always continue to reflect that era and also that it never become so exclusive that it would not be affordable to "common folks."

I visited the lodge and the springs on a sunny fall morning. Wakulla Springs Lodge reminds me of a palatial Spanish hacienda. The first thing that catches my eye when I walk into the lobby are the cypress ceiling beams with Aztec-style hand-painted designs on them. Blue and gold Spanish tiles frame the entranceway. The floors are mauve, red, and gray Tennessee marble tiles in a checkerboard pattern. A giant fireplace, made from native limestone and trimmed in marble, dominates the far wall.

A long glass case at one end of the lobby contains the stuffed and mounted remains of Old Joe. His plaque reads, "Old Joe's first and only cage." The most interesting room in the lodge is just past Old Joe's case—the soda fountain shop. There is no bar in the Wakulla Springs Lodge. Instead, Ball, who was fond of ginger whips (ice cream, ginger ale, and whipped cream), had a sixty-foot-long solid marble soda fountain counter installed.

After having a steaming bowl of navy bean soup for lunch (one of the dining room's specialties), I walk down to the springs. From the top of a twenty-foot-high diving platform, I look down on bream and bass schooling on the bottom. The water is amazingly clear. If not for a light breeze rippling the surface, it would look like a giant sheet of glass. It's no wonder that Hollywood came to this location to film Tarzan features and movies like *Around the World under the Sea*, *Airport 77*, and *The Creature from the Black Lagoon*.

DIRECTIONS: Take State Road 61 south from Tallahassee, and go east on State Road 267.

DON'T MISS: Old Joe

ADDRESSES AND EVENTS: See page 150

ST. MARKS

Population: 307

*W*HICH CAME FIRST—State Road 363 or Posey's Oyster Bar in St. Marks? I'm not sure, but if the oyster bar predates the highway (which runs straight south from the State Capitol for twenty miles, then dead-ends a half block from Posey's), then my guess is that some shell-fish-loving legislators had something to do with the road's construction.

St. Marks sits in the fork at the confluence of the Wakulla and St. Marks Rivers. The two combined waterways then flow another three miles south into the Gulf of Mexico. This has been a strategic location to lots of different people throughout history. It was an important village to the Apalachee Indians in 1528, when Spanish explorer Panfilo de Narvaez ran into them on his trek toward Mexico. The Apalachees gave him and his men such a scare that they hastily built rafts and took to the sea for the remainder of their journey (Narvaez and most of his crew drowned during violent storms on the Gulf before reaching Mexico). In the early 1600s, Spanish missionaries built the Mission San Marcos de Apalache (hence the name St. Marks), because they felt it was important to convert the Indians to Christianity. In 1680, Spanish troops thought that the location had strategic military importance and built the wooden Fort San Marcos de Apalache. Over the next two hundred years, the fort was alternately rebuilt and occupied by Spanish, French, British, and eventually American troops, when, in 1819, General Andrew Jackson seized it following the conclusion of the first Seminole War. Some remains can still be seen at the fort's site just off State Road 363.

The town of St. Marks was incorporated in 1830, and it became an important shipping port. The Tallahassee Railroad Company built one of the state's first railroads, from Tallahassee to St. Marks, in 1837. Mules pulled the cars. Today that route has been converted into the sixteen-mile Tallahassee-to-St.-Marks Historic Trail, a Rails-to-Trails project.

In 1929, Birdie Coggins convinced her husband Steve and friend T. J. Posey that the three of them should open a riverfront restaurant in St. Marks. They called it the City Cafe, and it gained rapid fame as the best seafood joint in this part of the state. Tallahassee politicians, including a succession of governors, were regular customers. Important deals were made over baskets of fried fish and Birdie's famous (secret recipe) hush puppies.

The City Cafe closed in the late 1940s, but T. J. Posey reopened it a few years later as Posey's Oyster Bar. Posey was an important man in St. Marks, becoming a member of the Wakulla County Commission and St. Marks City Council, and serving as judge and eventually as mayor. A year after Steve Coggins passed away (1965), Birdie married Posey and was back in the restaurant business for a while. Sometime around 1970, carnival operator Bill Helson bought Posey's (and kept the good name), and in 1989, Walter and Nancy Beckham, along with Walter's brother Donny, bought it from Helson.

Posey's Oyster Bar, a two-story, white-with-green-trim wood-frame building, backs up to the St. Marks River. From the front it looks identical to photographs taken of it in the 1930s when it was the City Cafe. The only difference I can see is that the signs now read, "Posey's Famous Smoked Mullet" and "Home of Posey's Topless Oysters." It's still a seafood restaurant (although you can get chicken or a burger or a corn dog, if you insist), and it's still famous. Naturally their specialty is oysters, and you can have them in any combination: raw or baked with butter, garlic, cheddar cheese, parmesan cheese, bacon, and, of course, cocktail sauce, horseradish, and lemon.

It's a weekday afternoon, but the place is busy. Nancy Beckham takes a short break to talk to me. "Walter and Donny come from a long-time oystering family, so they know their shellfish. This place is always hoppin'. Lots of regulars drive down from Tallahassee. We get folks who graduated from FSU twenty-five years ago and who stop in here every time they pass through, just for the memories."

Florida State University students still pack Posey's on the weekends, when they have live bands, and it's still a popular place with the Tallahassee political set. Burt Reynolds, an FSU graduate, is a frequent customer—and sometimes Jerry Reed comes with him.

When I suggest to Nancy that she should look into getting Posey's listed on the National Register of Historic Places, she replies, "That's something I've thought about. Come take a look at what I found in the closets when we bought this place." She leads me up a narrow flight of stairs to an attic-like room above the restaurant. It's filled with old chairs, dressers, and boxes of someone else's belongings from half a century ago. An antique bar takes up one corner. "Most of this furniture and stuff belonged to Birdie and Steve or Birdie and T. J." She hands me a big heavy wooden mallet. "This was T. J.'s gavel when he was judge, and this was his houndstooth hat." Stacks of framed pictures and photo albums sit gathering dust.

Nancy opens the doors to an old wardrobe that contains suits and dresses from another era. She carefully removes a pink evening gown. By the look in her eye, I can tell that this is the most prized of the items she found up here. "Birdie was just a little bitty thing—not more than five feet tall. She wore this gown to the Governor's Ball, probably sometime in the 1930s." She sighs and tells me, "If I had the time, I could turn this place into a museum."

Eating oysters and going fishing are the two main reasons people come to St. Marks, but there is more to see. The St. Marks National Wildlife Refuge, just four miles east (go back up to Highway 98, then take State Road 59 south), is home to a wide variety of coastal woodlands wildlife, from anhingas to alligators. The St. Marks Lighthouse, at the south end of State Road 59 in the Wildlife Refuge, was built in 1829. The eighty-foot-tall stucco-over-brick structure had to be moved back from the encroaching sea in 1841. Confederate troops were stationed here during the Civil War.

DIRECTIONS: Take State Road 363 south from Tallahassee until it ends.

DON'T MISS: Posey's Oyster Bar. Don't worry—you can't miss it.

ADDRESSES AND EVENTS: See page 150

JASPER

Population: 2,099

M OST SMALL TOWNS HAVE A GATHERING PLACE, the kind of place where, if you fail to check in with established regularity, folks begin to wonder if you've taken ill or something: 'Old Henry hasn't come in for breakfast in a couple-a days. Wonder if he's taken to feeling poorly?' The kind of place where, if you're an out-of-towner who has stopped in while passing through, the regulars will have learned the better part of your life story before you leave—and you'll have learned a good bit of theirs.

The H & F Restaurant in Jasper is one of those places. Open seven days a week—breakfast and lunch only. There's no menu; it's always a buffet.

I first heard about it from a friend, Margaret Hartley. "There's this great little Southern diner in Jasper . . . ."

Say no more.

My travel companion, Loretta Jordan, and I walk in around 11:15 Sunday morning just ahead of the church crowd. I am commenting on how good the vegetables look, and a gentleman in the buffet line ahead of us turns and asks politely, "Ya'll's first time here?" And a conversation commences.

It's not just the vegetables that look tasty. Everything on the buffet stirs my appetite. The ancestors of most of the long-time locals in Jasper—like those in nearly every small north Florida town—are from Georgia, Alabama, and South Carolina. The food here reflects that heritage: fried chicken, sausage, roast beef and gravy, turnip greens (with lots of ham hock), yellow squash, fresh pole beans, okra and tomato, butter beans, corn bread dressing (my favorite item), and dessert (bread pudding and three kinds of cake: strawberry, pineapple, and coconut).

"H & F is Handy and Frana. That's my Mom and Dad," owner Maureen Riley tells me. "They started the place. Been at this same location since 1968. Having it all-buffet makes it easier to operate, plus folks can better choose what they want to eat when they're looking right at it. There's a hunting reserve near here, so we get lots of hunters in here during the season from all over north Florida and south Georgia. Then there're the regulars we get in here day in and day out. They're all like family."

We sit down at one of the family-style tables with our heaping plates. "Where ya'll from?" And a conversation commences.

DIRECTIONS: Take Hamilton County Road 6 east from Interstate 75.

DON'T MISS: The corn bread dressing at the H & F Restaurant

ADDRESSES AND EVENTS: See page 151

KEATON BEACH,
DEKLE BEACH, AND
ADAMS BEACH

Population: Adams Beach 0; Dekle Beach 200 (estimated);
Keaton Beach 400 (estimated)

*I*N THE VERY EARLY MORNING HOURS OF MARCH 13, 1993, the
third most devastating storm ever to hit the continental United States
made landfall on the north end of Florida's Big Bend area. Its strongest
winds struck the tiny coastal communities of Dekle Beach and Keaton
Beach, where 10 people were killed and 150 homes were severely dam-
aged or destroyed (only 2 houses in Dekle Beach were left unscathed).
The total loss for the entire state of Florida would end up at 26 lives,
18,000 homes, and over $500 million in property damage. Over the
next couple of days, the storm would continue across the state and all

the way up the east coast, turning into a horrific blizzard. Because the storm hadn't formed as a traditional hurricane does, it wasn't given a name—despite record storm surges and winds well over one hundred miles per hour. Most simply remember it as the "No Name Storm of 1993." Those who experienced it refer to it as "The Storm of the Century."

On the map, Adams, Dekle, and Keaton Beaches appear as three little dots in a row on Taylor County's coast. I pick up Highway 361 off US 19 just south of Perry. Highway 361 carves a narrow path west and then south through unpopulated pine forest and eventually cypress marsh as it approaches the coast. This is not "coast" in the conventional Florida sense. There are no natural beaches. The woods and wetlands grow right up to the edge of the usually calm waters of the Gulf of Mexico. They call it the Nature Coast. Adams is the northernmost of the three. In the 1860s, it was called Jonesville, and there was a salt collection and processing plant here that supplied Confederate troops during the Civil War. Now it is simply the place where a spur road off Highway 361 (Adams Beach Road) dead-ends at the Gulf. When I walk down to the water, I can look both up and down the coast and not see a single sign of human intervention. It is strikingly majestic. This is probably pretty close to what it looked like to the Timucuan Indians (the original, pre-Seminole inhabitants of this region).

A few miles south of Adams, I roll into Dekle Beach, where one fishing pier and several docks occupy the shoreline, and three or four dozen homes sit atop towering stilts. It looks like they had a contest to see who could build the tallest stilt house. Most of them are thirty or forty feet above the ground.

A few more miles south of Dekle, I reach Keaton Beach, which is a little larger than Dekle Beach. Keaton Beach sits on property originally owned by a sawmill and turpentine businessman named Captain Brown back in the mid-1800s. Brown liked his bookkeeper, Sam Keaton, so much that he named the little community after him. Keaton Beach has a motel, a small marina, Hodges Park on the tiny man-made beach, and the Keaton Beach Hot Dog Stand right across from the park.

The Keaton Beach Hot Dog Stand is "the hot dog stand at the edge of the world." It seems such an anomaly, way out here. A gargantuan,

Keaton Beach Hot Dog Stand-the hot dog stand at the edge of the world.

menacing-looking shark's head hangs outside over its entrance. Inside it's a cozy eatery with picnic tables and benches, where they serve more than just hot dogs: fresh seafood, steaks, chicken—whatever owners Martha and Bill Hargeshiemer feel like throwing on the grill that day. The hot dog stand has been here since the mid-1970s—it was called Ruth's back then. Martha and Bill bought it in 1985 when they moved up from Plant City.

I order a barbecue pork sandwich and the requisite hot dog with the works—ketchup, mustard, pickle relish, and diced onions—at the window counter that opens into the kitchen. While Martha and Bill are fixing my meal, I ask them about the storm.

"Well, we had a roof left," Bill tells me, "but that was it."

Martha pulls three photo albums out from under the counter and passes them over to me. "There are some pictures in these," she says. "I was here when it hit. Bill was down in Tampa. Around six o'clock on the twelfth [March 12, 1993], I called the Coast Guard station down at Horseshoe Beach—they are about thirty-five miles south of here—and asked, 'Is it getting bad?' We have a lot of commercial fishermen in this area, so weather is a constant concern. The Coast Guard station tells me,

'Maybe sixty-mile-per-hour winds and two-to-four-foot seas.' Nobody knew what was coming. It hit like a freight train around three-thirty in the morning [March 13, 1993]. We had one-hundred-ten- to one hundred-twenty-five-mile-per-hour winds. The storm surge brought flood waters eight to ten feet high here—it pushed water inland all the way up to the curve in the road [about a quarter mile in]. Houses floated up off their foundations. At Dekle it reached as high as seventeen feet. That's why all their new houses are built up so high. It continued to blow until about eight o'clock in the morning. Rescue crews spent the next two days removing bodies from the tops of trees over in Dekle."

I thumb through Martha's photo albums, looking at before-and-after photos of houses and buildings and reading newspaper accounts of the havoc dispensed by the storm.

Bill calls me to the counter when my sandwich and hot dog are ready. Perhaps to change the subject to something more light, Martha asks if I would sign their guest book. It contains more than three thousand signatures and hometowns. Travelers from as far away as South Africa, Italy, Norway, and Great Britain have signed the book. Former President Jimmy Carter, his family, and his bodyguards all signed it in December 1994 while on their way to Steinhatchee for Christmas.

I finish off my sandwich and hot dog—which are both very tasty, by the way—then walk across the parking lot to Hodges Park and the beach. A commemorative plaque dedicates the park to the memory of those who died in the storm and to those who survived. Reading the plaque is sobering: it lists the names and ages of the Taylor County residents who died. Four were children. Repeated last names indicate that whole families were wiped out.

Keaton Beach and Dekle Beach have long since rebuilt, but the memory of March 13, 1993, will stay forever with their residents.

DIRECTIONS: Take State Road 361 southwest from US Highway 19 (south of Perry).

DON'T MISS: Keaton Beach Hot Dog Stand

ADDRESSES AND EVENTS: See page 151

FERNANDINA

Population: 8,765

WHEN I'VE MADE A MISTAKE, I figure it's best to admit it up front. Besides, maybe a preemptive acknowledgment will beat my critics to the punch. With that in mind, I have a confession to make. In my introduction to *Visiting Small-Town Florida* (Volume 1, Pineapple Press, 1997), I misjudged the town of Fernandina Beach, and I owe its residents and my readers an apology. I had commented:

"There are a few notable towns absent from this book, like Tarpon Springs and Fernandina Beach/Amelia Island, in spite of their rich histories, wonderful restaurants, and interesting museums. I've left them out because they have been encroached on by larger population centers.

Tarpon Springs is now surrounded by the Palm Harbor/New Port Richey megalopolis, and Amelia Island is becoming a suburb of Jacksonville. This clashes with the spirit and intent of *Visiting Small-Town Florida*, which is to offer you places where you can get away from the hordes."

I was trying to explain why I had left these otherwise—marvelous small towns out of the book. Tarpon Springs has been surrounded by a sprawling population (in spite of this, it is still a wonderful place to visit—fantastic food and a rich Greek heritage), but I was wrong when I said the same about Fernandina Beach. While Jacksonville's population (672,971 in 1990) has overflowed to Duval County's borders (in 1967, the City of Jacksonville and Duval County consolidated into one entity, making Jacksonville the largest city, in land area, in the world), it has yet to spill across the Nassau River Sound into Nassau County.

If the population were to spill over, at best it could only be at a trickling rate, because the only way to cross (on State Road A1A) from the south is via the Mayport Ferry. Two dollars and fifty cents is the price of passage onto Amelia Island.

Running north to south, Amelia Island is thirteen miles long and about two miles wide at its widest point. State Road A1A continues up through its center, past sand dunes, salt marshes, and scrub oak hammocks. There is no sign of development for a couple of miles until the road passes by the very ritzy Amelia Island Plantation resort. In a few more miles it veers northeast and continues up the Atlantic coast to the town of Fernandina.

It is October, and one of the Atlantic Ocean's late-season howlers is whipping up the surf. I am standing on the sea wall where A1A gets its last, northernmost look at the ocean. A few wetsuit-clad warriors are taking advantage of the ten-foot swells. Behind them, the sky is turning charcoal. I watch the surfers battle the waves for a few minutes, then I head west across the island on Atlantic Boulevard.

Atlantic Boulevard becomes Centre Street when it reaches the Fernandina Historic District. I turn south on 3rd Street, one block off Centre, to the Florida House Inn, where I have reservations for two nights. The Florida House Inn is Florida's oldest continuously operating hotel. It was built in 1857 by the Florida Railroad Company, owned by

David Yulee, Florida's first U. S. Senator. The Florida Railroad Company built Florida's first cross-state railroad, which ran from Fernandina (construction began in 1856) to Cedar Key (completed in 1861). As you will see, Fernandina is a place of many Florida "firsts" and "oldests."

Owners Bob and Karen Warner have restored and continue to maintain the Florida House Inn in its nineteenth-century grandeur. There are eleven rooms (two are suites). Some have fireplaces, and a few have old-fashioned claw-footed tubs. My room is at the top of the stairs. It has a four-poster bed and a ceiling fan and is decorated as if it were the master bedroom in the home of an antique collector. A plate of chocolate fudge sits on my night stand.

I am contemplating whether to have that fudge now or wait until after dinner, when I hear scratching at my door. Maybe someone has the wrong room and is trying his key in my lock. I open the door, and a blur of orange fur darts past my leg and under the bed. I later find out that this is Tatty, the Warner's tabby cat. Tatty does a five-minute inspection of the room, purrs her approval to me, then saunters down the hall. How's that for charming and homey?

I wonder who might have slept in this room over the years. In the decades following both the railroad's and the hotel's completion, the Florida House Inn was the place to stay. It hosted many dignitaries: President Ulysses S. Grant stayed here, and Jose Martí—renowned Cuban patriot during the Spanish-American War—was a frequent visitor, not to mention an assortment of Carnegies, DuPonts, and Rockefellers.

It's a half hour to the next dinner seating, so I follow Tatty down the hall and out onto the second-floor verandah, which extends most of the length of the inn. Tatty continues her rounds, but I stop and pull up a wicker chair to watch the coming line of rain move across the Victorian neighborhood.

Eight flags fly from the verandah's railing—one for each country or group that has claimed ownership of Amelia Island (more than any other location in the United States). First came the French. Huguenot Jean Ribault was the first European to set foot on Amelia Island (which he named "Isle de Mai") in 1562. This didn't sit well with the Spanish, since Juan Ponce de León had claimed all of Florida for Spain when he

The 1885 C. W. Lewis Tabby House in Fernandina has walls built of tabby, a poured mixture of oyster shells and cement.

landed just north of present-day St. Augustine in 1513. So, in 1565, the Spanish sent Pedro Menéndez de Aviles to kick the French out of Florida and off Isle de Mai, with great success. They renamed the island "Santa Maria."

Later there were invasions from the British—the earliest around 1702—but the island remained a Spanish territory until the first Treaty of Paris ended the Seven Years' War in 1763, and Britain returned Cuba to Spain in exchange for all of Florida. British General James Oglethorpe gave Santa Maria its new name, "Amelia," after the daughter of King George II. But the British underestimated how unfriendly the Indians could be, how much swamp land there was, and how many mosquitoes, snakes, and alligators there were in Florida, so twenty years later England traded Florida back to Spain. In 1812, a small group of U. S. patriots who called themselves the "Patriots of Amelia Island" over-threw the Spanish on the island and raised their own flag for a very brief time. In the summer of 1817, Sir Gregor MacGregor seized control of Spain's recently completed island fortification, Fort San Carlos. MacGregor flew his "Green Cross" flag, but withdrew a short time later. A few months after that, French pirate Luis Aury raided the island and raised the Mexican flag—unbeknownst to Mexico, by the way. By December of that year, U. S. troops had taken over the island and were holding it in trust for the Spanish. In 1819 Spain and the United States signed a treaty: the U. S. got Florida in exchange for taking over $5 million in debts that Spain owed the citizens of the United States. It took two years to iron out all the details, but in 1821 the United States officially acquired Florida and consequently Amelia Island from Spain. In April 1861 Confederate troops occupied Fort Clinch at the north end of the island, but Federal troops regained it a year later.

Like most Florida rain showers, this one rolls through quickly. The setting sun has found a gap between the horizon and the storm cloud's ceiling—a good time for me to wander around the historic district before dinner. Centre Street is generously landscaped with palms, oaks, and neatly manicured hedges. Gas lamp–style streetlights stand over brick crosswalks at each intersection. All of the street's late-nineteenth-century, mostly-brick buildings have been meticulously restored and are filled with shops, galleries, and restaurants.

The Palace Saloon, at the northwest corner of 2nd and Centre Streets, has operated continuously since German immigrant Louis Hirth bought the building in 1903. It had been constructed in 1878 as a haberdashery. The Palace is Florida's oldest operating saloon (another oldest!). Even if you are a teetotaler, you should visit this lavishly decorated establishment. There were plenty of bars in Fernandina around the turn of the century, but the Palace was considered the "ship captain's bar"— a hangout for the elite. I push open the Old West–style swinging doors and step back in time ninety years. I can easily picture Vanderbilts, Rockefellers, and DuPonts toasting their good fortune alongside sea captains and sailors on shore leave in here. The sixteen-foot-high ceilings are ornately formed from pressed tin—popular in nineteenth-century architecture but a lost art today. A forty-foot-long, hand-carved mahogany bar stretches the length of one wall. Mahogany caryatids support the mirror behind the bar. Larger-than-life oil murals, painted by

Roy Kennard in 1907, hang on the opposite wall. One features Dickens' character Mr. Pickwick; another, Shakespeare's Falstaff—famous beer drinkers, I presume. Apparently Roy Kennard returned to the Palace in the late 1950s and touched up all of his original work.

It was the railroad that turned Fernandina into a thriving place in the mid- and late-nineteenth century. Originally the town was located about three quarters of a mile north of its present location. In the 1850s, David Yulee promised its residents prosperity if they would agree to move the community south—closer to his railroad terminus and port on the Amelia River. They agreed, and Fernandina's Golden Era began. In a short time, luxury steamers from the North began bringing wealthy vacationers to Amelia Island. Luxury hotels were constructed, both in town and on the beach. Palatial Victorian mansions went up on the streets north and south of Centre Street. Fernandina's naturally deep harbor allowed large ships into its port, and the lumber, cotton, turpentine, phosphate, and naval stores shipping and rail transport industries boomed. The Spanish-American War in 1898 generated even more shipping and rail business. Not only had Yulee kept his promise, but the results of his efforts exceeded everyone's expectations. For nearly fifty years, the new Fernandina was both a world-renowned resort and a center of commerce.

During this time, Standard Oil mogul and railroad tycoon Henry Flagler set his sights on Florida. In the 1880s, he began building resort hotels along Florida's east coast. As they were completed, he would string them together with his railroad. Flagler bypassed Amelia Island, choosing not to connect with Yulee's railroad line. As a result, by the early 1900s, Fernandina's tourist trade had moved south to St. Augustine (Flagler's Ponce de Leon Hotel) and to West Palm Beach (Flagler's Royal Poinciana Hotel). Fernandina's flourish fizzled almost as quickly as it had begun. Had Flagler chosen to bring his rail line through Fernandina, Amelia Island may well have turned into a Manhattan Island South. The Victorian-era homes and Centre Street brick buildings would then, no doubt, have been replaced with larger and more modern structures. We can probably thank Henry Flagler for saving, in a very roundabout way, the Fernandina that we know today.

From the Palace Saloon, I walk another block west to the Fernandina

Beach Railroad Depot, just across the railroad tracks from the boat docks. Built in 1899, it replaced Yulee's original depot, which was demolished in an 1898 hurricane. The offices of the Fernandina/Amelia Island Chamber of Commerce are here now, and someone there gladly loads me up with history information, maps, and, of course, restaurant and lodging guides. Across from the depot is the stand-alone Duryee Building, named for William Duryee, the customs collector here in the 1800s. This was the first U. S. Customs office in America, built in 1882 (another first!). Since then it has been a bank and a newspaper office, and now it's the Marina Restaurant. I notice they're open early for breakfast, and I make a mental note to return in the morning.

Back at the Florida House Inn, I walk in just in time for the 6:30, every-half-hour dinner seating. Dinner is included in the night's stay. The dining room has long tables that seat a dozen each, and meals are served family-style. The group at my table engages in lively conversation while passing huge bowls of home-cooked Southern food back and forth. I scoop out a big spoonful of everything that passes by me—creamed corn, black-eyed peas, turnip greens. Next come the entree platters: fried quail, fried chicken, pork chops—I stab one of each (well, two of the quail). Corn bread, sweet tea, and chocolate cake with straw-berry cream cheese frosting round out the feast.

That evening the second wave of the storm blows through. The sound of rain pounding on the tin roof (and perhaps having eaten quite well at dinner) puts me to sleep early.

The following morning, I walk down to the Marina Restaurant. After a light French toast breakfast, I cross the railroad tracks to see the boat docks. The last remnant of last night's storm has passed, and fresh salty air cuts the ever-present aroma of the wood pulp/paper mills from the north. Commercial shrimping, fishing, and sailing charter boats rest moored at the pylons, each with its own pelican sentry.

Centre Street has a varied collection of shops, and I decide to check out a few of them. ZZ Toys, at 2nd Street across from the Palace Saloon, is a kid's (and not-yet-grown-up adult's) favorite, with kites, model trains, and wooden Brio toys. Centre Street Treasures, For the Love of Ashley, and The Cross-Eyed Bear are interesting gifts and collectibles shops. The Unusual Shop is appropriately named, with Caribbean wall-hung relief sculptures made from steel drums, cut out with a mallet and chisel then brightly painted. Celtic Charm is music, books, and hats—all from Ireland. A Touch of England has fine English bone china and an assortment of foods usually found only in the British Isles. I spend a good hour in the Book Loft Bookstore. One of their specialties is cookbooks from all over the South. They have Junior League cookbooks (always the best) from Charleston, Mobile, Atlanta, and elsewhere. Plus, they have a great collection of pirate books.

I head over to Third Street and then south a couple blocks to the Amelia Island Museum of History. On the way I stop at Main Squeeze, a tiny outdoor fruit juice bar on Third just south of Ash Street, for a fresh-squeezed grapefruit juice. The Museum of History occupies the old Nassau County Jail House, originally built in 1878 and remodeled in 1935 into the brick version it is today. The building was still a jail until 1975. The Museum took it over in 1986. The museum has a wonderful collection of maps, documents, and artifacts—some that predate recorded history and many from the seventeenth and eighteenth centuries. I find quite a bit of the historical information for this chapter there. Caretakers also conduct guided tours of historical Fernandina and offer specialized field trips—their tour of Amelia Island's cemeteries looks most interesting.

There's more history to be found at Fort Clinch State Park on the northern tip of the island. The road through the park turns north off Atlantic Boulevard, a few blocks in from the ocean, then winds through a tunnel of myrtle oaks. Thirty-foot-high sand dunes separate the road from the beach. Fort Clinch—named for General Duncan Lamont Clinch, who served during the Second Seminole War (1835–1842)— was built in 1847 (additional construction continued for several decades) by the United States to protect Cumberland Sound. No battles were fought here, but it was occupied by Confederate troops in 1861 and 1862 during the Civil War. Federal troops reoccupied it following General Robert E. Lee's order to withdraw. It was activated again during the Spanish-American War in 1898. Captain J. F. Honeycutt was given its command, but he found the fort half buried in sand and overgrown with cactus and weeds. Worse than that, the fort was infested with rattlesnakes. Honeycutt's crew spent most of their brief tenure restoring the facility to livable and usable condition. The State of Florida bought the fort in 1935 and began restoring it. Its last military occupation came during World War II, when the Coast Guard set up a station here.

Now Fort Clinch appears as it did during the Civil War. Park rangers dressed as Union soldiers reenact the daily lives of soldiers garrisoned here in 1864. I find a group of visitors in the infirmary (in the interior compound) who are listening to a Civil War medic describe his duties and his surgical tools. "This little spring device is my third pair of hands—I place it in an open wound, and it holds the tissue back so I can get to a broken bone or a bullet. Here's a jar of 'medicinal' whiskey and a jar of iodine. When I run out of iodine, I use creosote." Next he spreads out an assortment of menacing-looking chisel-like devices in various sizes. "These are my joint separators. It's much easier to do amputations with these than it is with a saw." In another room, a young girl is baking bread over an open fire and offers slices to passersby.

The surrounding walls of the five-sided fort are four-and-a-half-foot-thick brick with tabby (concrete and shell) reinforcement. Ramps lead from inside the fort to the tops of the walls. Ten enormous cannons, placed atop the two walls that face the water, guard the sound. From here I have a terrific view of the shrimping fleets heading out to the Atlantic and of Cumberland Island across the sound (and across the Georgia state line).

In the afternoon, the rain returns and prevents me from getting all of the photographs I want. I'm also going to miss taking an aerial tour of the island in a biplane with Island Aerial Tours. I vow to come back. Four months later, in January, I do.

This time I am staying on the beach at the Elizabeth Pointe Lodge, a half-block south of Atlantic Boulevard. Elizabeth Pointe's twenty-room main lodge, with its faded gray shingles, looks like an old turn-of-the-century Cape Cod mansion, but it was just built in 1992. The lobby, breakfast room, and sitting room look out across the Atlantic and are decorated in a nautical motif. The adjacent two-room Miller Cottage and four-room Harris Lodge architecturally match the main lodge. My ocean-facing, upstairs suite in the Harris Lodge has its own verandah and a boardwalk that leads across the low sand dunes to the beach. I'll be here for only two nights, but it would be a more-than-comfortable place to stay for two weeks.

Walking up and down the numbered side streets in downtown Fernandina, I pass an amazing assortment of restored, late-nineteenth-century homes, a few of which have been turned into bed-and-breakfasts. Some of the best examples of these homes are on South Seventh Street and on North Sixth Street. The Bailey House (now a bed-and-breakfast), at the northeast corner of Ash and South Seventh, is a beautiful example of Queen Anne architecture. Its two octagonal turrets, one large and one small, extend to the third floor. Some of the windows are stained glass. Completed in 1895, it took three years to build. Effingham Bailey, a steamship company agent, and his wife, Kate, were the original owners. The house remained in the Bailey family until the early 1960s. The C. W. Lewis "Tabby" House, directly across from the Bailey House on South Seventh Street, was built in 1885. Tabby, a poured mixture of oyster shells and cement, was used to build the walls. The rough texture

Elizabeth Pointe Lodge, a Cape Cod–style mansion bed and breakfast on Fernandina Beach.

doesn't accept paint well, so it's left in its natural, brownish-gray state. The mint green Addison House, across from the Tabby House on Ash Street, is another perfectly restored home that is now a bed-and-breakfast. It was built in 1876. Rumor has it that the privately owned, two-story brick house next door to (north of) the Tabby House is haunted. It is the third of the three-in-a-row Thompson Houses—named after Florida Senator William Naylor Thompson, whose relatives occupied the three houses.

Two blocks further south on Seventh Street I reach the Fairbanks House. George Fairbanks was a Confederate Army major who later became editor of Fernandina's *Florida Mirror* newspaper. The house is a colossal three-story, Italianate estate. The grounds take up half of the block between Beech and Cedar Streets. Fairbanks commissioned famous architect Robert Schuyler to design it, and history books report that he had it built as a surprise for his wife. Apparently Mrs. Fairbanks was not pleasantly surprised, and the house became known as "Fairbank's Folly." Theresa Hamilton, new owner with her husband, Bill, of the Fairbanks House, isn't convinced that's how it really happened.

She explains to me, "Just look at the size of these closets—and the number. Look at the layout of the kitchen. A woman was involved in the design of this house, and I think it's likely that it was Mrs. Fairbanks. The house was built in 1885, at the height of Fernandina's 'Golden Era.' This was the most opulent of quite a few mansions that were being built during that time. My guess is that there might have been some jealousy in the neighborhood when this house was going up. Rumors get started, stories get told."

As a bed-and-breakfast, the estate has three rooms in separate cottages and nine rooms in the main house—one that includes the fifteen-foot-high, third-floor tower. Most of the rooms have their own fireplaces and Jacuzzi tubs.

On both my trips to Fernandina, I find wonderful food—from the Florida House Inn's Southern-style dinner, to Elizabeth Pointe's delicious breakfast buffet (included with the room), to Fernandina's Fantastic Fudge on Centre Street (great pralines). On my first trip, I had dinner at Le Clos, a small French restaurant in a quaint yellow cottage on Second Street. My meal consisted of crusty, hot-out-of-the-oven

French rolls, excellent crab cakes with pineapple relish, and fresh-caught flounder sautéed in lemon, butter, and tomatoes. Owner/pastry chef Katherine Ewing made the rich chocolate cake—swimming in cherry sauce—that I devoured for dessert.

On the first night of my second trip, I have a bowl of crab soup, blackened scallops, and key lime pie at the Crab Trap Restaurant—all very tasty. My dinner companion, Loretta Jordan, has a grouper sandwich and saves the last bite for me (it is equally tasty). The Crab Trap occupies the bottom floor of the restored Seydel Building, one block north of the Palace Saloon. In 1876, a fire swept through the north side of downtown Fernandina and destroyed a number of wood-frame buildings. This was one of the brick replacements that went up in 1877. The Seydel Brothers, who came from Germany, lived with their families upstairs and ran a general store and millinery shop downstairs.

The Crab Trap is a casual place. The tables have disposal holes in their centers for sweeping crab, shrimp, or oyster shells off the table. Our waitress tells us a story about a boisterous Florida–Georgia football crowd whom she waited on one night. They decided to use the table hole as a basketball hoop and tossed everything—ketchup bottles, salt and pepper shakers, silverware, and beer mugs—into the hole. Note the fishing net draped across the length of the ceiling that clearly displays its turtle-excluder. Also, among the many stuffed fish hanging on the wall is one gargantuan, over-14-foot-long, 880-pound blue marlin caught off Kona, Hawaii, by Fernandina resident Michael Holland in 1988. The plaque says he caught it in an hour and 10 minutes on 80-pound-test line.

The following night's restaurant turns out to be not only one of the best small-town Florida restaurants I've dined in, but perhaps one of the best restaurants I've ever been to—anywhere. That's a strong statement, I know, but the Beech Street Grill (at Beech and Eighth Streets) is that good. For an appetizer, I have backfin blue crab cakes with tomato salsa. It has large hunks of tender crab and is superb. I then sample a fresh mixed-greens salad with toasted pecans, blue cheese, and mustard-basil vinaigrette dressing, and my entrée is grilled swordfish with a sweet mango-sake glaze, braised Chinese bok choy, and rice. The swordfish is the lightest, flakiest, freshest, most delicious I've ever had. Loretta has grilled tenderloin fillet with red-chili bernaise sauce and Jarlesburg custard potatoes (I sample both, and they are great). For dessert (I know, I should be stuffed by now), we split the flourless chocolate truffle torte with raspberry sauce, strawberries, and whipped cream. "Exquisite" is the only word that will do this fudge-density dessert justice. If you eat at only one restaurant when you visit Fernandina, make it this one.

A highlight of this second trip to Fernandina is a ride in Bill Rataille's 1929 open-cockpit WACO biplane. "Captain" Bill operates Island Aerial Tours at Fernandina Beach Municipal Airport. Bill, a retired building contractor who looks the Waldo Pepper–barnstormer type, tells me, "I love to fly, and there's no prettier place to do it than here. My WACO came equipped with a ninety-horsepower engine. I swapped it out for a two-hundred-and-twenty-horsepower version. You'll see why when we take off." Loretta and I don leather hats and goggles, climb up on the bottom wing, and drop down into the two-passenger compartment under the top wing. Bill pilots from a separate compartment directly behind us. The big radial engine pops and rumbles to life, and we motor out onto the grass alongside the paved runway, which he doesn't use. He quickly tests the rudder and ailerons then throttles up. We take two small hops across the grass, and in about 150 feet we are airborne! That's what the 220 horsepower is for. There is nothing to compare to the experience of flying with the wind whistling past your ears in a vintage open-cockpit airplane. We are sailing along, five hundred feet above the beach, when Bill rolls the biplane over to one side to give us a better view. He taps me on the shoulder and points out the Elizabeth Pointe Lodge. We've asked for a flight over pristine Cumberland Island to the north, and in a matter of minutes we are over Cumberland Sound. Once again, Bill is tapping our shoulders and pointing down. There is a U. S. Navy submarine base just north of Amelia Island, and our timing is perfect as we fly over one of their atomic submarines heading out to sea. On Cumberland Island we see wild horses and the ruined remains of Dungeness Mansion, built in the late 1800s by Thomas Carnegie (brother of Andrew).

On the return leg, Bill does two steep-turned passes over Fort Clinch while I click off a roll of film. (Check out one of my aerial photos in the color section.) Then we fly over Fernandina's port and the downtown district. Bill had told us that, if we liked, he would do a "lazy eight" on the way back to the airport. Now he's signaling us with his hand like an orchestra conductor. Oh, yeah, the lazy eight. I give him a thumbs up. Bill pulls the nose up skyward, then just before stalling, rolls left and dives down! Yahoo! As he builds up speed, he levels out, pulls the nose up vertical again, then cartwheels to the right and dives back down to the earth. It's a roller coaster ride without the tracks! In a few more minutes, we touch down lightly on the grass at the airport. It is a fitting end to a visit to what is now one of my favorite places in Florida.

DIRECTIONS: Go just north of Jacksonville on Highway A1A.

DON'T MISS: Fort Clinch, the Beech Street Grill, Island Aerial Tours biplane ride

ADDRESSES AND EVENTS: See page 151

CRESCENT CITY

Population: 1,859

US ROUTE 17 NORTH OUT OF DeLAND is a scenic, albeit leisurely, alternative to the concrete monotony of Interstate 95. This is fern-growing country, and the mesh tarp-covered fields are plentiful along the way. I'm coming into Crescent City, which rests atop a bluff on the curved (hence "crescent") west bank of Crescent Lake.

The first families settled here in 1852, and a few more came in the late 1860s following the Civil War. In 1875 Charles Griffing bought most of the property and divided it into single-acre home lots and five-acre citrus groves. Griffing's wife, Jennie, changed the name of what was then Dunn's Lake to Crescent Lake, because its shape reminded her of the crescent moon. The new town adopted the name of the lake.

US Route 17 becomes Summit Street when it passes through downtown Crescent City. I turn east on Central Avenue and follow it four blocks downhill to Crescent Lake. Docks with covered boat houses line the shore. This lake, like many others, once claimed to be "the bass capital of the world." However, Crescent City's big annual event is the Catfish Festival held in April. The agenda includes bluegrass music, arts and crafts displays, and a parade, but the highlight is the catfish skinning contest. There are some interesting turn-of-the-century houses and buildings here. One is the 1892 Sprague House Inn, now a restaurant and bed-and-breakfast. Unfortunately, they're closed today so I can't get in, but the mostly-seafood menu looks enticing.

Back at the top of the hill, at the intersection of Central Avenue and Summit Street, Total Interiors, an antique and gift shop, occupies a nicely restored, two-story brick building. On the Central Avenue side of the corner, this building connects with a quaint, tin-roofed, wood-frame house with a white picket fence and a big mulberry tree in the front yard.

1892 Sprague House Inn and Restaurant on Central Avenue in Crescent City.

Around the corner on Summit, I walk into Native Traditions Gallery, an interesting shop with Southwestern art and jewelry—lots of turquoise, lapis, and silver. Owner Gary Street tells me, "We lived down in south Florida for a while and became so frustrated with the traffic and crowding that we began looking for a better place to live. When we came to Crescent City, we knew this was what we were looking for." Gary carries a lot of Native American items from New Mexico and Arizona, and he tells me that he is beginning to carry some made by Florida (Seminole) Native Americans. On my way out, he gives me a sprig of dried sage that has a marvelous aroma, and he suggests, "Tear off one leaf at a time. Let it burn on a plate—it will fill the whole room."

Even without burning, the sage fills the interior of my Isuzu Trooper with its pleasant scent to complement the pleasant scenery as I leave Crescent City.

DIRECTIONS: North of DeLand on US 17.

DON'T MISS: Native Traditions Gallery

ADDRESSES AND EVENTS: See page 153

CENTRAL REGION

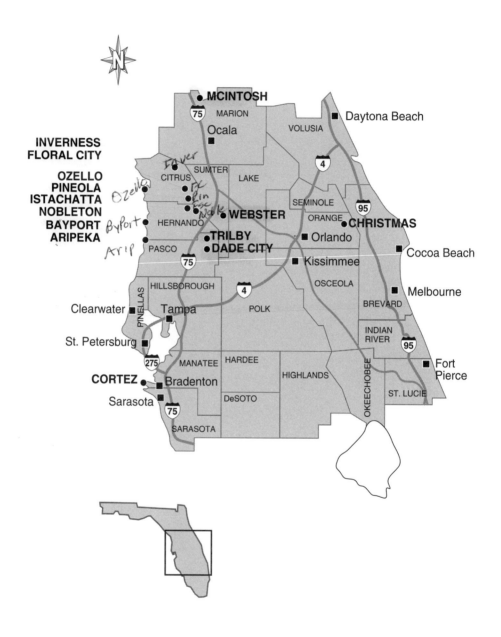

INVERNESS
FLORAL CITY

OZELLO
PINEOLA
ISTACHATTA
NOBLETON
BAYPORT
ARIPEKA

MCINTOSH

MARION

75

Ocala

VOLUSIA

Daytona Beach

Faver

SUMTER

CITRUS

LAKE

FK

Lin

ise

No'k

Ozella

HERNANDO

WEBSTER

SEMINOLE

ORANGE

CHRISTMAS

4

95

Orlando

ByPort

TRILBY

DADE CITY

Arip

PASCO

75

Kissimmee

Cocoa Beach

OSCEOLA

HILLSBOROUGH

4

Melbourne

BREVARD

Clearwater

PINELLAS

Tampa

POLK

INDIAN
RIVER

St. Petersburg

95

275

MANATEE

HARDEE

Fort
Pierce

HIGHLANDS

CORTEZ

Bradenton

OKEECHOBEE

ST. LUCIE

Sarasota

DeSOTO

75

SARASOTA

MCINTOSH

Population: 411

MY GOOD FRIEND AND FORMER BROTHER-IN-LAW, Jack Hardy, has insisted since I first began my research on *Visiting Small-Town Florida*, Volume 1, "You should check out McIntosh. It's a scenic and historic little town and fits perfectly with what you are searching for." Jack, a University of Florida alumnus, never misses a Gator football game and knows every back route (and each stop along the way) between Tampa and Gainesville. He's probably driven through McIntosh a hundred times.

Better late than never, I am traveling north on Highway 441 between Ocala and Gainesville. The road rises to the crest of a ridge, and then suddenly I have a sweeping view to the east across open pasture land, across Orange Lake and beyond. Although I can't see it, I know that Marjorie Kinnan Rawlings' home at Cross Creek is about five miles due northeast on the far bank of Orange Lake. Just north of this pastoral panorama, I roll into the quiet hamlet of McIntosh. At Avenue G, the town's only traffic light (a blinking one), I turn right.

Huge live oaks grace every yard, their Spanish moss-covered limbs spreading out over the tops of homes and across streets. They must be centuries old. Some have trunks as big around as small houses (and look as though Keebler elves live inside them). I've never seen so many grand oak trees in one place. Two of the grandest are in the front yard and backyard of Margie Karow's Merrily Bed and Breakfast on the south side of Avenue G.

The Merrily is a yellow, two-story Folk Victorian, with a steeply pitched tin roof and black shutters. W. E. Allen, McIntosh's first post-master, built the house in 1888. Margie must have a green thumb. Ferns, flowers, and caladiums fill her entire yard.

Most of the other houses along McIntosh's Avenues (B through H) are also 100-plus-year-old Victorians—some restored, some not. They were originally the homes of citrus and cotton farmers whose fields surrounded the town. After the big freezes of 1894 and 1895, the farmers switched to vegetables—watermelon, crookneck squash, cabbage, lettuce. I'm told that the old Gist House, at the corner of Avenue H and Fifth Street, was built with the revenues of a single season's crookneck squash crop. Another farmer grew iceberg lettuce exclusively for the ocean liner Queen Mary and shipped it by train to New York.

A few blocks past the Merrily, at the end of Avenue G, I come to McIntosh's restored railroad depot. Originally constructed in 1884 by the old Florida Southern Railroad, it was scheduled to be torn down in 1974. In 1973, a group of townsfolk who felt the depot was a valuable landmark formed the Friends of McIntosh to try to save it.

McIntosh postmaster Sharon Little is one of the original founders and the current president of the Friends of McIntosh. She moved here in 1972 and became postmaster in 1981. Sharon is working the counter when I walk into the post office (a block from the depot).

"We formed the Friends of McIntosh in 1973 just to save the depot,"

Sharon explains. "We needed to purchase it from the railroad and move it six feet back from the track. Six thousand dollars is what we had to come up with, and we decided that the best way to raise that would be to hold a little festival right here in the park. Our first 1890s Festival was in 1974. We had twenty-five vendors and drew about thirty-five hundred people."

The 1890s Festival has run every year since, on either the third or fourth weekend in October (so as not to conflict with a Gator game). It now draws forty thousand people and features tours of McIntosh's historic homes, storytelling, a parade, over three hundred vendors, and all-day live entertainment.

Back out on Highway 441 (at the blinking light), I stop to visit Village Antiques in an old two-story, clapboard building with a red antique phone booth out in front. No modern arts-and-crafts stuff filling the shelves here. It's all genuine (as in "old") antiques—furniture, jewelry, china. In one corner at the back of the store, there's Dr. Ray Giron's Ft. McIntosh Armory and Civil War Museum—an amazing collection of antique uniforms, swords, firearms, and documents. Some of it predates the Civil War. One display case features items from the War of 1812. Giron also supplies props for Civil War movie productions, and that's what he's doing today. In the other corner, Gordon Lambert has set up his McIntosh Clock Repair shop. Clocks of every size, shape, and style—most of them antiques—sit on shelves and in cases or hang from the walls. While I watch Gordon reassembling a pile of tiny gears and springs at his work table, all the clocks suddenly begin chiming at once—top of the hour. I jump about three feet high! Gordon doesn't even flinch.

Two blocks north I stop at O. Brisky's Book Barn. I'm familiar with O. Brisky's because I've visited their excellent used book store in Micanopy (about seven miles north of here) many times. The Barn in McIntosh, however, is more than just a book store. They sell all kinds of antiques—furniture, figurines, curios, and some quite old books. The barn itself, built around 1900, was originally a citrus packing house for the Brown Packing Company.

Manager Virginia "Ginger" Blinn is on the front porch, restitching an antique quilt pillow, when I walk up the steps. She tells me she'd be glad to tell me what she knows about McIntosh if I don't mind her talking while she works. Ginger has lived in McIntosh since 1981. She previously worked as a park ranger at the Marjorie Kinnan Rawlings State Historic Site in Cross Creek, so she has a keen interest in the area's history. She also has some insightful things to say about how a small town tends to include all its residents, how it sees to it that every individual counts.

"I thought, when I first moved here, that I would simply live in this little town while my husband attended law school. It turns out you don't just live in a little town. You begin to get to know the people who live here, and they get to know you. Right away, they feel out what you have a knack for, and they don't let you just sit on that gift. They expect you to use it. Every person has worth here."

In the 1930s and 1940s, as the more fertile land in south Florida began to be cultivated, farming around McIntosh faded. Today it is primarily a bedroom community for people who work in Ocala (seventeen miles south) and in Gainesville (seventeen miles north). Without any new industry moving in after the 1940s, McIntosh never experienced a surge in new housing. At the time, things may have been bleak, but the long-term blessing-in-disguise is that most of the turn-of-the-century Victorian houses were not torn down, leaving McIntosh the tranquil and historic village that it is today.

"McIntosh is small, intimate, and looks and feels like a place where time stands still," Ginger says.

Don't think that means that McIntosh is stagnant. While the population has stayed at around four hundred for the past century, it is always dynamic—with a constant renewing cycle of generations. Ginger tells me, "This is a place where people stay. When we first moved here, there were eighteen widows. The women had married men twenty years older than they were—when the men died, the women lived on in these big old houses. As those older women died, the homes were bought by young families. Now children are back in McIntosh. It's refreshing to see a community revitalize itself with young people. McIntosh has the kind of lifestyle that was more commonplace forty, fifty, sixty years ago: where it's safe for children on the streets; where there are five churches [in a town of only four hundred]; where there's a community center that is genuinely active; where Boy Scout leaders have been leading for forty-seven years; where the old and the young still rub shoulders."

Ginger's observations echo the feelings of people I've met in so many small towns. She states those feelings very eloquently: "McIntosh offers quiet, a sense of security, and a sense of home. In this world, people are searching for that—it's not an easy thing to find anymore. Now, don't think that this is some sort of 'land over the rainbow.' We have our fusses and politics like any other town, but there's also more interplay between the members of the community. When you live in such close proximity—and everyone knows you—you have to be responsible for whatever your position is or your actions are, like towns of a hundred years ago, when there was censure by the community itself. It makes you think twice about what you're going to say or do, and I think that's healthy."

I think that this closeness, this "everyone-pulling-together"ness is one of the reasons that so many people are moving to small towns. Ginger agrees. "They are clamoring for it. Especially people who are raising families. Small towns like McIntosh are becoming very alluring. We've gone through this era of suburban sprawl and the scattering of the American family. And now there's a real desire to have our children experience something different, something a little more stable. A small town feeds you in ways that I don't think a big town can. What it really does is it gives you back the family, something that we [society today] don't have enough of."

Thanks for the insight, Ginger. Thanks for the suggestion, Jack.

DIRECTIONS: Take exit 72 off Interstate 75, follow State Road 318 east to U. S. Highway 441, and go north.

DON'T MISS: O. Brisky's Book Barn

ADDRESSES AND EVENTS: See page 153

INVERNESS

Population: 5,797

*A*T FIRST, INVERNESS TOWNSFOLK FEARED THAT THE WIDENING of US Highway 41—and the consequential bypass of their downtown Main Street—would be the equivalent of cutting off the blood supply to a limb. Happily, the opposite happened. Thanks to a committee of local business people, instead of succumbing to a withering death, downtown Inverness got an injection of new life. Its one-block-long Main Street, with the historic Citrus County Courthouse marking its east end and the twenty-foot-tall Bank of Inverness clock at its west end, is now a vibrant district with restaurants, galleries, and shops.

I park my car and go for a walk to take an inventory of Main Street's businesses. Stumpknocker's Restaurant, Angelo's Pizzeria, and Cat's Gourmet Coffee House offer a variety of dining options. Among the assortment of shoppers' choices are Vanishing Breeds (a gift shop and boutique with an endangered animals theme), Inverness Antiques, It's All Art, and Ritzy Rags and Glitzy Jewels, where I meet Andrea Perry, who shows me her latest acquisition: two handmade (one from bamboo and sterling, the other from carved bone and sterling) medicine carriers from the Flores and Sumba Islands in southern Indonesia. No doubt they were procured by some Indiana Jones type and if opened might unleash an ancient spell or curse!

Around the curve on Courthouse Circle, I walk into Alternative Gallery and Gifts. Artist Carl Lundgren owns the gallery, which doubles as his studio. "I display and sell the art of Florida artists in a variety of media. Naturally, a lot of their work is of Florida subjects. The back half of the shop is where I do most of my own work." Carl's oil paintings depict fantasies but are startlingly lifelike and show an Old Masters-like appreciation for light, shadow, and the human form.

Gas lantern–style street lights blend well with Main Street's restored buildings and storefronts. The brick, three-story, neoclassical-revival Masonic Lodge Building at the corner of Main and Pine Streets was considered a skyscraper when it was constructed (for $17,285) in 1910. The Masons of Lodge #18 used the third floor and leased the first floor to retail shops and the second floor to a dance and theater production group. Today the restored building once again has retail shops downstairs. The Citrus County Board of County Commissioners, a real estate office, and a law firm occupy the upper floors.

The old yellow-brick 1912 Citrus County Courthouse, which replaced the original 1892 wood structure, has been in restoration since 1994 under the supervision of the Citrus County Historical Society. Ed Cole, a Historical Society volunteer for eleven years, tells me, "It's been a painstaking process. First, we had to peel off all the layers that had been added over the decades: paneling nailed up over interior walls, drop ceilings, partitions, carpet, paint. What we found underneath was the beautiful work of skilled craftsmen and masons. Let me show you some of what's been done."

Ed leads me carefully around saw horses and ladders. Down one hall, carpenters are sanding and varnishing some of the original woodwork trim. Workers have uncovered the first floor terrazzo floors and marble wainscoting. Transom windows that had been painted over and nailed shut are being refinished and rehinged so they will be functional again.

Old photographs of the courthouse gave some clues to what the hidden walls, floors, and ceilings looked like, but seeing them revealed after so many years must have been exciting. Society members and architects even watched old reels of the 1961 Elvis Presley movie *Follow That Dream*. The closing courthouse scene was filmed in the second floor courtroom, and everyone saw what the room looked like more than thirty-five years ago. (Much of the movie was also filmed in Yankeetown. For more information, see the Yankeetown section in *Visiting Small-Town Florida*, Volume 1.)

The Citrus County Historical Society's offices, archives, and museum are housed in the courthouse, although lately they have had to shift everything from room to room to keep clear of reconstruction. Nonetheless, they are happy to turn me loose in a room filled with filing cabinets and boxes of documents and books—a treasure trove of

The very regal and very British Crown Hotel in Inverness.

items from and information about Citrus County's past.

The rough-and-ready Tompkins brothers, post–Civil War Confederate soldiers, settled here in 1868. They called it Tompkinsville. Records show that the name changed to Inverness in 1889. Local legend claims that an emigrant Scotsman (whose name no one can recall) became homesick while standing on the banks of Lake Tsala Apopka (adjacent to Tompkinsville/Inverness). It reminded him of the lake country near his home, Inverness, Scotland. At least one report claims that the Scotsman was one of the many phosphate-boom speculators who swarmed to north-central Florida in the late 1880s and early 1890s and that he offered to donate two thousand dollars toward the construction of a new courthouse if they would change the name of the town.

In 1887, the newly formed Citrus County had designated the nearby town of Mannfield as the temporary county seat. Four years later, a county election decided that Inverness would be the permanent county seat—much to the disappointment of the residents of Mannfield and to the consternation of Senator Austin S. Mann, who developed Mannfield. W. C. Zimmerman (then-clerk of the circuit court) refused to deliver the county records to their new location and also to vacate the old Mannfield office. He sat at his desk while the entire office was removed from around him and loaded on a wagon. Finally, the sheriff and a contingent of deputies loaded Zimmerman, still in his chair, onto the wagon along with his desk and boxes of records and transported all to the new offices in Inverness. Accounts I have read say that Zimmerman continued to record minutes throughout the trip. Inverness went on to become a center of commerce while Mannfield became a ghost town. Zimmerman became the Citrus County Superintendent of Schools.

Many of Inverness' buildings and houses from its prosperous turn-of-the-century era are still in use. Some have been restored. One of the most impeccable restorations I've seen in all my small-town research is Inverness' Citrus High School, now the administration building for Citrus Memorial Hospital. This red-brick, two-story building, with a bell tower over its entrance, was originally built in 1911 and restored in 1992. Photos on the corridor walls chronicle the thorough reconstruction.

Some other interesting and historic structures are the 1910 Clark

House at 314 West Main Street, now a Coldwell Banker Real Estate office; the 1900 Hicks House at the corner of Tompkins Street and Osceola Avenue (Robert Hicks built this unusual octagonal house to withstand hurricanes, and it is still in the Hicks family); and the 1901 Carter House at 301 West Main Street, with its hexagonal corner gazebo, now offices of the *Citrus Times* (an edition of the *St. Petersburg Times*).

My favorite Inverness historic building is also my accommodation for tonight, the Crown Hotel. This white, three-story, wooden structure, with burgundy canvas awnings over its windows, reminds me of a Scottish country club. But the now-dignified inn had humble beginnings. The Crown began life as a general store when Alf, one of the Tompkins brothers, gave his brother-in-law, Francis Dampier, property on which to build a store. Dampier built the store on one side of the street and his home on the other side. Sometime around 1900, Dampier moved his store from Bay Street to Main Street, and in 1907 he turned it into a boarding house called the Orange Hotel. Ten years after that, he sold it to a New York hotel syndicate, which moved it again in 1926, this time around the corner to Seminole Avenue, its present location.

In conjunction with the move, the New York group performed what must have been an amazing feat of construction in its day: They built an entirely new bottom floor, then hoisted the original two-story building up into the air and placed it on top of the new first floor to make a three-story hotel, which they named the Colonial.

The Colonial was a popular place for a number of decades, but by the 1970s it had fallen into serious disrepair. It had recently been condemned when, in 1979, Reg Brealy came to Inverness, representing the British company Epicure Holdings. The company had sent Brealy to look at another piece of property, but he convinced them that the Colonial was the real diamond-in-the-rough. They bought it for a reported $100,000 and spent the next year and a half (and an additional $2,000,000) completely restoring it in fine English-residence style. Epicure Holdings renamed the structure the Crown Hotel and also built a new restaurant and kitchen and added a swimming pool.

The Crown is everything a British inn should be: regal, stately, and elegant, with an interior decorated in forest green, burgundy, and, of course, royal blue. A crystal chandelier hangs from the ceiling in the lobby atrium. A wide, curving, one-piece floating staircase sweeps around the chandelier up to the second floor landing. Lithographs depicting British countryside hunting scenes hang from hallway walls. Beneath the stairs, a glass case displays an exact replica of the Crown jewels. Epicure Holdings purchased the set from one of the few British companies licensed to reproduce the gems.

Office manager Terrie Adkisson has worked at the Crown Hotel since its grand reopening in 1981. She recalls the restoration. "It was a total reconstruction. Except for a few items like antique light fixtures, everything that went in was new. This beautiful wood staircase was custom built in North Carolina and shipped in one piece. It arrived the same day as the chandelier."

The hotel even had its own authentic 1909 double-decker bus—an Inverness landmark that sat parked in front of the Crown for many years. "Epicure bought the double-decker bus at an auction in London and had it shipped to Portsmouth, Virginia," Terrie tells me. "One of the gentlemen who was going to help with its restoration flew up to Portsmouth, then drove it all the way down to Inverness—in the middle of winter! The bus is right-hand drive. The driver's compartment is completely open—there's not even a windshield. And it ran at a top speed of about thirty-five miles per hour! Last year [1997], we donated it to the city. They are re-restoring it, and it will be on permanent display on a new brick bus pad that will be built downtown."

Epicure sold the Crown Hotel in 1985, and then it sold again in 1990 to the current owners, Nigel and Jill Sumner. The Sumners, originally from Manchester, England, operated a seaside hotel in Wales before moving to Inverness and acquiring the Crown. "The Sumners are hands-on, working owners," Terrie tells me. "At any given moment you might find her working down in the laundry room, and he might be washing dishes in the kitchen." The personal care they have taken with the hotel shows: The Crown exudes English fastidiousness.

The elegant Churchill's Restaurant on the first floor of the Crown Hotel is perhaps better known than the hotel itself. Regular diners come from as far away as Ocala and even Tampa just for Sunday dinner, according to Terrie. Friend and fine restaurant connoisseur Dr. Clyde

The 1911 Citrus High School building in Inverness was
meticulously restored in 1992 and is now the administration
building for Citrus Memorial Hospital.

Asbury once told me that you can always judge a restaurant by its soup. If the soup is exceptional, so will be the rest of the meal. This is indeed the case at Churchill's. I start my dinner with the chicken and rice soup, which sounds rather ordinary but is not. It is creamy and thick, almost chowderlike, well spiced and filled with carrots, celery, potatoes, and large tender chunks of chicken breast. Then for an appetizer I have rumaki-chicken liver wrapped in bacon, baked, and, in this case, floating in a savory mild brown sauce. My entrée is decidedly British and exceptionally tasty: braised veal kidneys and steak tenderloin, sautéed in onions and bacon, with a rich bourbon gravy. Fresh green beans and a baked potato round out the plate.

For lunch the following day at the Crown's Fox and Hound Pub, I have split-pea soup and curried chicken over wild rice with chutney, sliced almonds, raisins, and shredded coconut on the side. Don't let anyone tell you that the Brits prefer bland food—this meal was full of flavor. The menu features other traditional British fare, such as homemade English sausages with mash, cottage pie, and steak and kidney pie. The Fox and Hound's atmosphere and decor are, naturally, British/Scottish pub.

The forty-six-mile-long Withlacoochee State Trail (which runs roughly from Trilby in the south to Dunnellon in the north) was one of Florida's first "Rails to Trails" projects. The state bought the rail right-of-way, which was no longer in use, and converted it into a state park trail. The State of Florida Park Service bought this stretch from CSX Railroad in 1989. It comes to its approximate two-thirds point in Inverness and passes through just a couple of blocks north of the Crown. "The Trail brings us a lot of business," Terrie explains. "Bicycle tours regularly make the Crown their lunch stop or overnight stop."

I can best summarize Inverness as a picturesque and historic small town with a touch of old-world charm and class.

DIRECTIONS: Take U. S. Highway 41 north from Brooksville.

DON'T MISS: Crown Hotel

ADDRESSES AND EVENTS: See page 154

FLORAL CITY, PINEOLA, ISTACHATTA, AND NOBLETON

Population: Floral City 2,500 (estimated); Istachatta 93;
Pineola and Nobleton, fewer than 50 combined (estimated)

*E*ARLY SETTLER HUGH BOYLAND MUST HAVE BEEN CAPTIVATED by the profusion of wildflowers when he suggested the name Floral City for this picturesque village, which was officially laid out in 1883. The following year, Boyland contributed something else to the town: oak trees, which he planted in rows on each side of Orange Avenue (County Road 48). Over the past century, those trees have grown tall and wide and have crossed over the top of Orange Avenue, forming a quarter-mile-long tunnel known as the "Avenue of Oaks."

Like nearly everyone who passes through here, I have to stop at the crest of the hill on East Orange Avenue and take some pictures. The branches of these grand oaks reach clear across the road to intertwine with one another. I can't tell where branches from the south side end and those from the north side begin.

Aroostook Avenue, with its own rows of oak trees, forks diagonally northeast from here and dead-ends at the shores of Lake Tsala Apopka. This was a busy steamboat port where oranges, along with lumber and the occasional passenger, could be shipped via the newly completed (in 1884) Orange State Canal down the Withlacoochee River to the rail-head at Lake Panasoffkee. Aroostook Avenue was Floral City's original Main Street until the big freeze of 1894-1895 killed the area's citrus industry and ended the steamboat business. Fortunately, right about the same time as the big freeze, phosphate was discovered nearby. Mines opened up, and Floral City had a new industry.

This quaint town has an impressive collection of historic homes and buildings, some restored but most simply well preserved. Many were built during the phosphate boom (1890s-1910s), when Floral City's population swelled briefly to over ten thousand (due to the influx of transient mine workers). At least one house predates that era: The Formy-Duval House, at 7801 Old Floral City Road (which runs north and south a couple of blocks east of Highway 41), was built in 1865. It is the oldest house still standing in the area. John Paul Formy-Duval was a cotton, sugarcane, and citrus farmer who owned vast tracts of land— 342 acres of which would eventually become Floral City—surrounding the southern end of Lake Tsala Apopka.

The 1894 D. A. Tooke House, at 8560 Orange Avenue, and the 1910 J. T. Love House, next door at 8580 Orange Avenue, are two good examples of the Queen Anne Victorian architectural style. Both are large, one-story homes with twin steep-roofed gables. The simple wood-frame Floral City Methodist Church, at 8508 Marvin Street (a block north of Orange Avenue), has been in continuous use since its construction in 1884. The Cracker Victorian-style W. C. Zimmerman House, at 8441 East Orange Avenue, was built in 1890. (See Inverness chapter about W. C. Zimmerman.) The cedar-shingle-sided Soloman Moon House, at 8860 East Orange Avenue, was built in 1893. The 1904 William H. Dunn House, at 8050 South Bedford Road (on the west side of Highway 41 and several blocks south of Orange Avenue), is the boy-

1910 James T. Love House on Orange Avenue,
"Avenue of the Oaks," in Floral City.

hood home of well-known Florida historian Hampton Dunn. Hampton's nephew and his nephew's wife currently live in the house and are restoring it.

The two-story 1889 Commercial Hotel (also called the Magnolia Hotel) at 8375 East Orange Avenue—with its full-width front porch, leaded stained-glass windows, and triple-gabled roof—was originally the home of James Baker, son-in-law of John Paul Formy-Duval. Baker was one of the principal developers of Floral City. The house was relocated from two blocks away in 1895 and converted into an elegant hotel. Currently it is under renovation. A small, yellow, concrete-block building attached to its west side houses Carlotta's Antiques. When I walk in, owner Carlotta Yancy is putting up new inventory. I've been keeping an eye out for an interesting Mother's Day present, and I find it here: a family of four ceramic, hand-painted bears. Mom collects bears to decorate her Highlands, North Carolina, condominium. Carlotta tells me that these pieces "were made by ceramic artist Howard Pierce, probably in the 1940s, at his studio in Claremont, California. Pierce's style is easily recognizable because of his unusual [for that era] airbrush painting."

Floral City's largest business is citrus grower Ferris Groves. Doc Ferris started his orange grove business in 1927, when he took over property on Duval Island (in Lake Tsala Apopka) on which his father had originally intended to build a golf course. Ferris reintroduced citrus to the area after its forty-year absence. In 1940, Ferris built a packing plant and a roadside fruit stand on Highway 41 just north of Orange Avenue. In 1955, he built a permanent fruit store and gift shop which still operates today. It is reminiscent of the many tourist shops that sprang up in the 1950s and 1960s along Florida thoroughfares. After another hard freeze in the mid-1980s, the folks at Ferris Groves changed their focus to strawberries, for which they are famous today.

A note of Floral City trivia: A few of the town's residents were relatives of famous people. Doc Ferris was the grandnephew of George Washington Ferris, who invented the Ferris Wheel and introduced it at the 1893 Chicago World's Fair. One of Floral City's early (1880s) orange grove farmers, Jacob Clemens, was the cousin of Samuel Clemens (Mark Twain). Floral City resident Robert Dillinger (by all accounts, a mild-mannered fellow) was cousin to notorious 1930s gangster John Dillinger. Floral City's best-known native (and one of my favorite Florida historians) is Hampton Dunn, who now lives in Tampa.

I'm always looking for great little roadside diners, and I found one in Floral City. Lee's Coffee Shop has been in the same spot, just north of town on Highway 41, since 1964. Lee's is a time capsule from the 1960s. Owners Allen and Sherrie Richards have kept the simple decor the same as it must have looked thirty years ago. A sign in the window reads, "The quaint little place with the curtains." I make it in the door just a minute before closing at 1:00 P.M. (they're open for breakfast and lunch only). I can hear the Byrds singing "Mr. Tambourine Man" back in the kitchen. The grill is still hot, so I order a juicy, medium-rare cheeseburger with grilled onions and pickles, French fries, a lemonade, and a slice of homemade pumpkin pie with whipped cream for dessert.

Properly refueled, I head back south but instead of staying on Highway 41, I turn east once more on Orange Avenue (County Road 48). At Istachatta Road (County Road 39) I steer south. This book is

*Old dock at the Big Bass Fish Camp property on the Withlacoochee River
near an 1800s ferry crossing in Istachatta.*

supposed to be about small towns, but once in a while the roads that
run between them are worth mentioning. Istachatta Road winds
through some of the most scenic rolling hills, oak hammocks, and pastureland in this part of the state. At some points it parallels the
Withlacoochee State Trail. "Pastoral" is the word that comes to mind.

After six miles I ease into quiet Pineola, made up of a handful of res-
idences and an old cemetery next to the New Hope United Methodist
Church—one of the oldest churches in this area. Church founders built
the original New Hope Church out of logs on this site in 1830, then
replaced it with a wood-frame structure following a fire in 1886. In
1940 the congregation built the current church, reusing much of the
lumber from the 1886 building. Some of the hand-hewn pews are from
the original 1830 church. New Hope's annual October Homecoming
draws 150 past parishioners from around the state.

Another mile down the road and across the Hernando County line, I
come to Istachatta. The name has been variously interpreted as Creek

Indian for "red man" and "man's river crossing." There was a ferry crossing here on the Withlacoochee River in the 1800s that was replaced by
an iron bridge in 1910 (which is no longer there). Istachatta has a community park, a tiny library, and a post office. Next door, the Istachatta
General Store and Farm Supply building still stands, but it's been boarded up since the mid-1980s. Someone should turn this place into a bed
and breakfast. The Withlacoochee State Trail passes right next to it. On
the opposite side of the trail, on the cypress-lined shore of the
Withlacoochee, are the deserted remains of the Big Bass Fish Camp. An
inscription on the lone brick chimney reads, "From all the guys on
Saturday night."

Continuing south then east on Lake Lindsey Road (County Road
476) for about a mile and a half, I reach Nobleton, at the crossing of the
Withlacoochee River. The Nobleton Boat Rental Outpost, on the north
side of the highway, rents canoes, kayaks, and pontoon boats and gives
airboat rides. That's one half of Nobleton. The other half is the Riverside
Restaurant & Bar, on the south side of the highway. It's been only a couple of hours since my burger, fries, and pie at Lee's, but I spring for a
bowl of Riverside's chicken soup. I'm not expecting much, but it turns
out to be delicious—homemade with whole pieces of chicken breast,
rice, corn, green beans, carrots, and celery.

These four communities—three so tiny that each has fewer than a
hundred residents—still retain much of the old-Florida flavor, and I
hope that never changes.

DIRECTIONS: **Floral City:** Take US Highway 41 north from
Brooksville to Floral City.
Pineola and Istachatta: Take County Road 48 east to County Road
39 and go south to Pineola and Istachatta.
Nobleton: Continue south and then east on County Road 476 to
Nobleton.

DON'T MISS: Orange Avenue (Avenue of the Oaks)

ADDRESSES AND EVENTS: See page 154

ARIPEKA, BAYPORT,
AND OZELLO

Population: Aripeka 150 (estimated); Bayport 0; Ozello 200 (estimated)

"*U*SELESS 19"—THAT'S WHAT DRIVERS HAVE DUBBED the stretch of US Highway 19 from Clearwater north. It has been widened and overpasses have been built at crossroads, but it is still a frustrating experience to travel on this main Pinellas County/Pasco County artery—an artery that could use an angioplasty, in my opinion. It's not just the traffic that exasperates me: It's also the tacky suburban clutter that sprouts up alongside the highway, like the crabgrass that invades my front yard.

Not until well past Hudson does US 19 become "useful" again. Five miles further north, I turn west down Pasco County Road 595/Aripeka

82

Road. The contrast is dramatic. Pastureland replaces parking lots and gives way to pine woods and brackish swamps as I approach the small coastal port community of Aripeka, called Gulf Key when it was first settled in 1886.

Back then, visitors rode the Governor Stafford passenger steamer here for fishing and recreation. They stayed at the Osawaw Inn (now gone), built by the Aripeka Saw Mill Company. Gulf Key adopted its new name from the saw mill company. "Aripeka" is most likely a slight variation on "Arpeika," a Miccosukee Seminole chief who also went by the unlikely name of Sam Jones. In 1835, just prior to the Second Seminole War, then–Florida Governor Andrew Jackson mandated that all Seminole Indians must be removed from Florida and sent to reservations out West. Chief Arpeika was one of eight tribe leaders who refused to relocate their people. Instead, they fled south to the Everglades and established Sam Jones Old Town near present-day Fort Lauderdale. An alternate claim is that Aripeka is a mispronunciation of another Seminole leader's name, Apayaka.

Thankfully, Aripeka's rate of growth has been nominal over the past one hundred-plus years. It is still a quiet fishing enclave. A few stilt fishing shacks appear on my right as the road slows at a sharp S-turn before bridging the south fork and then the north fork of Hammock Creek. The Aripeka Fish Camp and Marina, a small bait-and-tackle and general store, sits between the bridges and backs up to the north fork. The faded wooden sign on the front depicts a palm tree, beach, and sunset paradise. It reads "Aripeka, Fla. 5.9 miles from Heaven." I stop in to get some refreshment and to survey the interior. Fishing lures, leaders, rods and reels, bait buckets, and long-billed hats hang on racks and occupy shelves alongside groceries. Several fishermen, already back from their early morning trip, are discussing how best to cook their coolerfuls. I place my breakfast—a carton of orange juice and a package of powdered doughnuts—on the counter and ask the manager behind it: What is it that's 5.9 miles away? He sneaks a glance at his fishing pals and then turns to me, "Five point nine miles to the best fishing spot in the Gulf, but I'm not saying in which direction."

I walk out to the bridge and watch two guys tossing cast nets off the side while I savor my breakfast. This is the heart of Aripeka. No motels.

No restaurants. Just a quiet place to cast a net or drop a line and soak up the beautiful natural Gulf Coast scenery. Well, quiet except for the airboats—the standard mode of transportation in these parts, more popular than pickup trucks. Actually the airboats are pretty quiet, too, as they glide under the bridge and up the creek at no more than idle speed. From here west, Hammock Creek spills out across a sawgrass delta and into the Gulf of Mexico. The view is idyllic and should be even more so at sunset. If Heaven is 5.9 miles out there somewhere, then this must be the Pearly Gates.

County Road 595 continues north from Aripeka and follows the shoreline for a couple of miles. It's difficult to tell where the sawgrass ends and the Gulf begins. This short stretch is quintessential "back roads Florida." After a while, 595 turns inland, then takes a left fork north again. When it runs into Highway 50, I follow that out to Bayport on a marshy point at the mouth of the Weeki Wachee River. The road ends at a picturesque park with a boat ramp.

Bayport was a lumber, cotton, and supplies port during the Civil War. Like many other small Gulf Coast ports, Bayport became vital after the Union's East Gulf Blockade Squadron succeeded in cutting off the larger Gulf Coast shipping ports. By 1864, Union troops felt that Bayport had become significant enough to invade it, too. For twenty years after the war ended, Bayport was a bustling town and the area's busiest port. Regularly scheduled wagon runs transported goods between here and Brooksville, but in 1885 rail service came to Brooksville, and Bayport's usefulness declined rapidly. Nothing remains of the town today, but the park and boat ramp are popular put-in spots for the Weeki Wachee River.

Back out on US Highway 19, I continue north and pass D. O. T. signs that warn drivers to watch for bears crossing. This is one of the few remaining habitats for Florida black bears.

Just north of Homosassa, I turn west on Citrus County 494/West Ozello Trail. For a mile or so, the road winds through a swampy forest. There's no shoulder: The palmetto scrub grows wild right up to the edge of the road. Intermittently, as I near the coast, the road opens up to sawgrass savannas dotted with cedar bayheads. The community of Ozello (the westernmost in Citrus County) is technically on an island,

The Masonic Lodge building in Inverness was considered a skyscraper by townsfolk when it was built in 1910.

Old Pittman Store across from Lawrence Grocery Store in Two Egg (population 28).

*The 1916 Overstreet Post Office/Patrick's General Store was moved to
Nicholson Farmhouse property near Havana in 1995.*

The 1885 Fairbanks House Bed & Breakfast in Fernandina was once the home of George Fairbanks, editor of Fernandina's newspaper, Florida Mirror.

The 1937 Wakulla Springs Lodge was built by DuPont Estate trustee Edward Ball.

Aerial view of Fort Clinch from Bill Rataille's 1929 open-cockpit WACO biplane.

Built in 1857, the Florida House Inn in Fernandina is Florida's oldest continuously operating hotel.

The 1926 Lacoochee School House was restored and relocated to the Pioneer Florida Museum in Dade City.

One of only seven remaining Stiltsville houses in Biscayne Bay just south of Key Biscayne.

1896 home of Dr. Cyrus Teed, founder of the Koreshan Unity in Estero.

*The Barnacle Bed & Breakfast in Big Pine Key is located on one of
the few natural beaches in the lower keys.*

North fork of Hammock Creek in Aripeka, originally settled as Gulf Key in 1886.

Boat docks in Fernandina, a town made prosperous in the 1850s by Florida's first U. S. senator, David Yulee.

separated from the mainland by tributaries of the St. Martin River, Salt Creek, and Greenleaf Bay. A million water passageways crosshatch this nether land, looking like varicose veins on the map. As in Aripeka, airboats are the transport of choice here.

Until 1955, Ozello Trail was an oyster-shell path with palmetto logs bridging the swampy sections. It frequently flooded out, but this was no deterrent to the local residents, who were accustomed to getting around by boat. From 1880 until 1943, Ozello's children daily paddled rowboats and canoes to their one-room schoolhouse on one of the many tiny hammocks in the bay just south of Ozello. They called it the Isle of Knowledge. The island is still there (south off the end of John Brown Road), but, unfortunately, the schoolhouse is gone.

Ozello Trail ends at the edge of the open Gulf and at Peck's Old Port Cove Seafood Restaurant and Blue Crab Farm. Calvin Peck has been harvesting blue crabs in specially constructed tanks behind his restaurant since 1982. Around back, I get to survey his operation. Hundreds of blue crabs fill fourteen tanks. One of the chefs is scooping up a bucketful of the scrambling critters.

Once inside, I order the specialty, garlic crabs, and I know they're fresh. The waitress promptly spreads two sections of newspaper across my table—my first clue that this is going to be no ordinary lunch. Next, she drops off a walnut cracker and a large empty mixing bowl. Then the crabs arrive in their own large mixing bowl. Steam billows from the heap of legs and claws.

Now, I consider myself to be an expert at cracking stone crab claws, but this is clearly something different. Stone crab claws are big. One claw can fill the palm of my hand, and they crack neatly when popped on their fattest part with the back of a heavy spoon. A blue crab's claws are smaller—about the size of my thumb—and the body is about the size of my hand. I don't want to look like a rookie, so I smile and tell the waitress, "Thanks. I'm all set!" I think I can figure out the claws and the cracker, so I start on those. It's a lot of work for a little bit of the very sweet crab meat, but it sure is delicious. After about five minutes, the waitress scoots past my table, and I catch her taking a quick, passing inventory of my bowl out of the corner of her eye. She does an immediate U-turn. "All right," I confess, "I'm managing on the claws, but I don't have a clue what to do with the bodies." It's her turn to smile. She grabs half a crab (they're already chopped in two), snaps it into two quarters, and in a flash, extracts a small hunk of meat with thumb and forefinger. This is obviously an acquired skill. I spend the next forty-five minutes trying to imitate her technique. I consume as much crab as I'm able to. The once-empty bowl is now piled high with carcasses, seemingly higher than the full bowl that I started with. This surprises me, since most of the crab remains appear to be stuck to the front of my shirt. This is the world's messiest eating task; barbecued spare ribs don't even come close. I head to the rest room to wash up, but what I really need to do is take a jog through a drive-through car wash.

My next stop is Windflowers Studio. I had passed the mint green house and yard filled with sculptures on my way to Peck's. My crab-cracking waitress insisted that I visit Maryann Winters and Gordon Benson at Windflowers on my way out.

Maryann and Gordon moved to Ozello twenty years ago on a motor-cycle trip. "Sold all our belongings at the flea market," Maryann tells me, while Cory, their tail-wagging schnauzer mix, sniffs hungrily at my shirt. "Came up here [from Clearwater] and rented a house. It's just so peaceful here. Quiet, except for weekends sometimes." What happens on the weekends? I ask. "Well, we get a lot of people like you. Now, I don't mean that in a bad way at all! Folks pass through, they stop, and they chat a few minutes. I usually send them to one of the county parks for a picnic or to fish. They come to sightsee, eat lunch or dinner, enjoy the scenery. We have the most beautiful sunsets you've ever seen in your life, right from the causeway across from Peck's."

A mountain of driftwood, mostly twisted arms of cedar, takes up the westernmost corner of the property at Windflowers. Sculptures depicting Florida wildlife—manatees, porpoises, ducks, pelicans, and herons—are scattered among a garden of flowers and hanging plants, conch shells, and nautical discards (old crab traps and floating markers, buoys, and pilings) turned into decorations. The yard is like some forgotten outdoor museum—a final resting place for objects long past their original usefulness. Old salvage finds a home here. "Gordon collects it, and I fix it up and sell it." Or sometimes she doesn't sell it, and it becomes another in the family of artifacts that garnish the yard. Maryann converted a bathtub into a fishbowl for a family of unusually large goldfish (she feeds them Grape-Nuts). A king-size antique wood headboard with a mirror is planted in the front yard and surrounded by flower beds. Cory's doghouse—decorated with old crab trap floats, assorted potted plants, and other adornments—mimics her owners' house.

Two items really stir my curiosity: a six-foot-tall scale model lighthouse, now rusted and leaning to one side, and the skeletal remains of an old wooden riverboat. "A friend gave us this old metal lighthouse. His dad had built it when he was a boy. He's in his fifties now, so it's forty-five-some-odd years old. I've had so many offers to buy it, but it's not for sale. I need to put it back together. That old boat came off the bottom of one of the canals. No telling how old it is." About twenty feet long, it has the appearance of something that has been submerged in water for a century, although the glass in its front window ports is still intact.

I ask Maryann where the pile of driftwood came from. "Gordon has collected that wood over the course of the twenty-plus years we've been here. It's mostly cedar. Actually, it's not driftwood. Years ago there was a pencil factory in Cedar Key, north of here. A lot of their cedar wood came from this area. This wood is leftover from when they cut the logs."

The factory she referred to was the A. W. Faber pencil mill, located on Atsena Otie Key a half mile offshore from Cedar Key. The Faber mill closed its doors in 1896 following irreparable damage from a hurricane. That makes Gordon's collected remnants over one hundred years old.

Maryann polishes the wood with a high-speed circular wire brush, then fashions it into a base for one of her ceramic creatures or a frame for a hanging sculpture. The back portion of the house is Maryann's shop (I would call it a factory). She has a variety of table saws and wood-working tools and shelves filled with molds and cans of paint. Plus, she has a kiln the size of a large, horizontal freezer for firing her ceramics.

Windflowers Studio might seem idiosyncratic anywhere else, but in Ozello it somehow fits right in.

On my way out of Ozello, I stop for a quick bite at the Wench's Brew. OK, it's a biker bar, but they have a surprisingly good restaurant separate from the bar with lots of fresh-out-of-the-Gulf seafood items on the menu. I start with their "soon to be famous" seafood chowder. It deserves to be famous—thick and creamy with whole jumbo shrimp, fresh grouper, clams, potatoes, and celery. Next I have their crab cakes with Dijon sauce. This place is good. Don't let the empty parking lot fool you: Most patrons arrive by airboat at the restaurant's own dock out back.

DIRECTIONS: **Aripeka:** Five miles north of Hudson, take County Road 595 west off US 19 to Aripeka.
Bayport: Continue north from Aripeka on County Road 595 to Highway 50, and go west to Bayport.
Ozello: Go west on Citrus County 494/West Ozello Trail off US 19 between Homosassa and Crystal River to Ozello.

DON'T MISS: Aripeka Fish Camp and Marina, Windflowers Studios

ADDRESSES AND EVENTS: See page 155

WEBSTER

Population: 746

I CAN SURE TELL IT'S MONDAY. I'm heading north on Highway 471, and although I'm still four miles south of Webster, I'm already seeing all the indications that today is flea market day. Garage sale signs, roadside stands, and vendors working out of the backs of vans and pickups line the highway.

Every Monday, the Sumter County Farmer's Market in Webster hosts Florida's largest and probably oldest flea market. Sumter County has always had an agricultural-based economy. Citrus was big here prior to the Great Freeze of 1894. After that, peppers, cucumbers, cabbage, lettuce, beans, and other vegetables became the staple crops. In the early 1900s, Webster was known as the "Cucumber Capital." In 1937, a group of local farmers formed a co-op and, without state funding or financial help from the county, built a market in the middle of Webster from which to auction their produce. The farmers built the facility themselves, harvesting cypress trees from nearby swamp lands and using mules to drag out the lumber. The Farmer's Market was then and remains today a not-for-profit operation. It is still owned and operated by the local agriculture businesspeople.

Over the decades the market evolved along with changes in local farming trends. A cattle auction (now the second largest in Florida) replaced the vegetable auction, and people began to sell other items out of the empty produce stalls. These days the cattle auction takes place on Tuesdays, and the flea market is on Mondays. When I inquire at the office about the flea market's schedule, a friendly lady behind the counter cheerfully gives me what must be her standard answer, "Fifty two weeks a year, unless Christmas comes on a Monday."

The enormous, forty-acre facility overwhelms me from the minute I walk through the market's gates. A dozen roofed, open-air walkways with hundreds of vendor stalls, plus several more enclosed buildings and open paved lots, house a total of over fifteen hundred vendors, who contract for their spaces on an annual basis. Except for occasional intermittent cancellations, there are no vacancies. Each space has been booked for years. This is a busy place with a carnival-like atmosphere. The market opens at 6:30 A.M. and closes at 4:00 P.M., and there's a crowd here most of the day. A sign at the entrance reads "No trespassing, except on Mondays."

The first booth I come to is Mary Ann's Kitchen, which has a wide assortment of put-up jams, jellies, and fruit preserves. There are some fruit names that I don't even recognize: What is a scuppernong? Jars of peach preserves tempt me to pull out my wallet right away. Instead, I decide to wait and get them on my way out. I don't want to have to carry them around with me all day. I can see myself in a couple of hours, wandering around this place with two arms full of goodies.

I don't want to miss anything, so I decide to approach this maze of merchandise systematically. I retreat to the southwest corner of the market, walk up the first row along the south perimeter, then back down the next, and so forth. They sell everything here, some of it new but most of it used. One person's discards are another's treasure—antiques, computer equipment, hunting knives, power tools, parakeets, flowers, jewelry, watches, musical instruments, golf clubs, grandfather clocks, comic books, old records, Barbie dolls (and all accessories), Matchbox cars, sports trading cards, coins, and stamps. If someone collects it, there's a vendor for it here. I see miracle kitchen appliances (The World's Best Vegetable Peeler!), and at one booth I find a 1956 juke box for $1,200. There are clothes and whole bolts of fabric, bicycles and baby carriages, Nintendo games and stuffed teddy bears.

My favorites are the two rows of stalls filled with fresh fruits and vegetables: peaches, plums, pears, peppers, squash, nectarines, tomatoes, onions. A wonderful fresh aroma floats up and down the aisles. Speaking of food, they don't want you to go hungry while you're here, so concessionaires sell the usual assortment of corn dogs, curly fries, and Italian sausage sandwiches. I resist these but can't get past a booth where a woman is selling caramelized cinnamon-roasted pecans. She cooks them—as I watch and drool in anticipation—in a superhot vat of melted cinnamon, brown sugar, vanilla, and some other ingredients "which we are not at liberty to divulge." They are heavenly—I think I could survive on nothing but water and these pecans for months. This treat has filled me up, so I reluctantly pass on sampling Grumpy's homemade ice cream, but I've heard from more than one source that Grumpy makes the best.

For several hours, I have been hiking up and down rows, weaving through booths, rummaging through tables, and wandering around stalls. I conclude that there are enough tools, equipment, artifacts, odds and ends, and other unclassifiable items here to build a house, decorate the interior, and fill the closets with clothes and the refrigerator with food!

Just before stepping out of the gate, I stop again at Mary Ann's Kitchen. This time I chat with Mary Ann Elliott. "OK, what's a scuppernong," I ask?

"It's a sweet yellow grape," she tells me. "They grow them in North Carolina and in north Georgia and make wine from them. The ones in my jam came from Georgia."

Mary Ann and her husband's stall consists of one table with her jars

Webster Flea Market: the largest, and likely the oldest, flea market in Florida.

of jams and jellies and six tables covered with every size, shape, and style of cowboy hat in existence. "We started here seven years ago with one small booth of hats, and it's grown ever since. I would always buy preserves and jams from other booths here at the market. Finally I decided to start putting up my own at home. They came out so good that we decided to start selling them."

I was going to get the peach preserves, but I became intrigued by Mary Ann's pear-honey jam. "I grind up the pears, mix them with sugar, and slow simmer the mixture, letting it cook down until it's thick. I add pineapple and cook it down some more," she explains. "When it reaches the right consistency, it goes in the jar. It's good on muffins, bagels, pound cake, ice cream."

Sold!

Across from the flea market on Highway 471, I drive up East Central Avenue to Webster's E. C. Rowell Public Library. E. C. Rowell's family moved to Webster in 1922. He was an Air Force pilot during World War II, and in 1965 and 1966, he was the Florida House of Representatives Speaker of the House.

Librarian Judy Lee shows me the library's Civil War Archives Museum, which has an interesting collection of artifacts, books, and old newspapers. One display case contains a Civil War–era saber, paper Confederate currency, and letters dated 1861—sent from Confederate soldiers to home. Another case displays a Civil War–era leather ammunition case, a carpetbag, a Confederate flag, and a cannonball. There is also a booklet that gives directions to nearby cemeteries containing Civil War graves.

Judy also helped me find books on Sumter County history. Many of the first settlers here paid for land with U. S. Government warrants issued to them for their service during the Seminole Indian Wars. Purchases with these warrants date back to the 1850s. In 1869, George Hayes opened a post office in the back of his general store. He submitted his application to the U. S. Postal Service with the community name Orange Home. The application came back rejected, with a note that said there was already an Orange Home elsewhere in the state. Hayes needed a quick alternative. He glanced at the dictionary on his desk and decided to borrow the name Webster.

Webster is very proud of its agricultural heritage. On the third weekend in May, the town holds its annual Pepper Festival as a tribute to local farmers. Peppers were a major crop in this area after the turn of the century. Locals compete in a log sawing contest, a horseshoe tournament, a riding lawn mower race, and a stuffed pepper cook-off. Live entertainment and lots of good food have made the Pepper Festival a popular one since 1991.

Before heading back south, I drive up to the Dade Battlefield Historic Site, which is northwest of Webster, just east of Highway 301 on County Road 476. A monument there marks the site where Chief Micanopy, head of the Seminole Indians, led his December 1835 attack on U. S. Army soldiers under the command of Major Francis Dade. Micanopy's warriors, who outnumbered Dade's men almost three to one, ambushed and killed over one hundred Army soldiers. Only three survived. The battle is known as the Dade Massacre. It was the first confrontation of the Second Seminole War, a conflict that started when U. S. troops tried to force the Seminoles to relocate to reservations out West. The war lasted until 1842. Ultimately, many Seminoles were sent

to Western reservations, but some evaded capture and fled to the
swamps of the Everglades, where their descendants still live today.

DIRECTIONS: Take Highway 50 exit (Brooksville) east from I-75 to
Highway 471, and go north.

DON'T MISS: What else? Sumter County Farmer's Market flea market
(Remember: Mondays only)

ADDRESSES AND EVENTS: See page 155

TRILBY

Population: 100 (estimated)

O N MY WAY HOME from Webster and the Dade Battlefield Historic Site, I decide to take a slight detour and stop at the tiny community of Trilby, at the crossing of Highway 98 and County Road 575. The centerpiece of Trilby is the "Little Brown Church of the South," now the Trilby Methodist Church. Charter church members and Reverend T. H. Sistrunk built this wood-frame, tin-roof structure in 1897 and 1898. The building, its tall steeple rising from the covered entranceway, was relocated a short distance to its present location in 1920. Next door, a historical marker explains that the 1870s settlement of McLeod changed its name to Macon in 1885 when the first post office was opened. In 1896, the name was again changed, this time to Trilby, after George DuMaurier's popular novel of the same name. Town officials named several of the streets and the town's Svengali Square after characters from the novel.

At one time, Trilby had a bank, a school, a railway station, two hotels, a saw mill, a grist mill, a grocery store, a dry goods store, a drug-and-sundries store with a soda fountain, and a tuberculosis hospital. In the 1920s, it was a busy little town. That all changed in one afternoon in May 1925. Townspeople first spotted smoke coming from the second floor of the dry goods store around 1:00 P.M. They quickly started a bucket brigade, taking water from the water tower at the south end of town. Dade City's fire truck rushed to the scene, but during the time it took to drive the eight miles, flames had consumed all of the buildings on the west side of the railroad tracks. By 5:00 P.M., firefighters had contained the blaze, but most of downtown Trilby was gone. Some was rebuilt, but the town never fully recovered from that tragic afternoon. Thankfully, one of the buildings left standing was the "Little Brown Church of the South."

DIRECTIONS: Take Highway 301 north from Dade City, then take left fork at Highway 98.

DON'T MISS: "Little Brown Church of the South"

ADDRESSES AND EVENTS: See page 155

CHRISTMAS

Population: 2,500 (estimated)

ON THE COUNTER AT THE POST OFFICE IN CHRISTMAS, Florida, there is a green ink pad and a box filled with rubber stamps to commemorate an assortment of holidays and special occasions. Patrons pick the appropriate stamp and adorn their envelopes. "Children love the stamps," post office employee Rose Harbeck tells me as she smiles from behind the counter. "They are always the most fun. When they come in to send packages to their grandparents or whomever, they always put all the stamps on them." The entire wall to my left is covered with Polaroids of kids with their cards to be mailed. A sign above the pictures reads "Future Philatelists" (stamp collectors).

I ask Rose if things get hectic here right before Christmas. "Hectic? Yes, but actually it's absolutely beautiful. The only people who would come all the way to Christmas, Florida, just to mail their cards and packages are people who really love other people. Why else would they go through that much trouble just to have "Christmas" on their postmark? So we really get to meet the finest folks. They come here from all over, many from Europe—while visiting Disney they hear about us."

Not only do people come by in person, but starting in November of each year, the Christmas post office begins receiving boxes of letters and packages to mail out with the Christmas postmark. This small post office becomes a busy clearinghouse for parcels coming in from around the world, then going back out around the world, often right back to where they came from. "We get some of our biggest boxes of letters from Germany, Italy, Spain, England, and Japan. Usually (people) include a letter to themselves as well—maybe to see if we've done a good job or not," Rose chuckles.

"This past Christmas [1997] *Good Morning, America* came, and they filmed all day long. They couldn't believe we had a spot out front to tie up horses. When they asked why we needed that, we explained that some folks around here come on horseback. They gave us a kind of funny look, you know. Then, sure enough, about that time a fellow rode up on his horse, tied it up, walked in, got his mail out of his P. O. box, then rode off. Those *Good Morning, America* people liked the Christmas postmark idea so much, they sent us a box of their cards to postmark."

The Christmas postmark looks pretty much like any other—an oval with "Christmas, Florida" across the top, the date in the middle, and the 32709 zip code across the bottom. In 1997, this little post office stamped and mailed out over 250,000 Christmas cards, quite a bit for an office that serves an area with a population of fewer than 3,000. "It starts to get crazy the day after Thanksgiving, but we love it," says Rose.

The current Christmas post office was built in 1987. Paintings on the wall depict the 1918 and 1937 post office buildings. The first post office was established in 1892 in the home of postmaster Samuel Hurlbut. His son, Van, delivered the mail twice a week on foot to as far away as Chuluota—twelve miles north.

Christmas was originally Fort Christmas. In only two days, United

*More than 250,000 holiday cards pass through the Christmas Post Office
each December to get the "Christmas" postmark.*

Fort Christmas reproduction at Fort Christmas Historical Park.

States Army troops, under the command of General Abraham Eustis, built the 80-foot-by-80-foot log fort with two block houses. They began construction on December 25, 1837—hence the name. It was one of many forts put up during the Second Seminole War (1835-1842). The original fort no longer stands, but there is an impressive re-creation, built in 1977, at the Fort Christmas Historical Park on Fort Christmas Road, two miles north of State Road 50.

DIRECTIONS: Take State Road 50 east from Orlando or west from Titusville.

DON'T MISS: Getting your Christmas cards stamped at the post office

ADDRESSES AND EVENTS: See page 155

DADE CITY

Population: 5,633

*T*WENTY-FIVE MILES NORTH OF TAMPA, the terrain begins to turn hilly as US Highway 301 rolls into Dade City, named for U. S. Army Major Francis Dade. Dade and his troops camped near here in December 1835, just days prior to meeting their demise at the Dade Massacre, which sparked the beginning of the Second Seminole War. (See Webster chapter.)

My first stop is Lunch on Limoges (known to regulars as L. O. L.) to put my name on their perpetual waiting list. I know people who drive all the way up from Tampa just to eat lunch here. Skip Mize and Phil Williams have operated their lunch-only restaurant since 1979. The restaurant is adjacent to Williams Fashions, a women's boutique and gift shop. Phil is the third generation of Williamses to operate what began as Williams Department Store in 1908.

The perfect Dade City day includes putting your name in at L. O. L. when it opens at 11:00, wandering around the downtown antique and gift shops for about forty-five minutes, returning for lunch, walking off lunch (and, believe me, you'll need to) by browsing at the rest of the downtown shops, then visiting the Pioneer Florida Museum on the north edge of town.

With my name securely on the L. O. L. reservation list, I venture out around the block. Dade City has a varied selection of shops spread over a dozen-block area. At the corner of Meridian Avenue and Highway 301, I walk into Glades Pottery and Gallery. They sell hand-thrown stoneware and porcelain pottery made right there in the shop. The open pottery studio takes up one quarter of the store, so I sit back and watch the potter at work. It's messy but mesmerizing: There is something hypnotic about watching a vase or bowl come to life as it spins on the table. The potter subtly works the whirling, wet clay until it achieves the shape he is looking for. It seems part craft and part therapy.

Around the corner on Meridian, I take in Tickle Your Fancy, which has lots of collectible stuffed teddy bears. Next door, the Sandbar Market has a nice collection of antique furniture and fixtures. I am particularly interested in some of their antique sewing machines. (I own a circa-1940s Singer 107W3 that I use for making and repairing parachutes, so old sewing machines catch my eye.) They have a 1925 Franklin, an old Japanese Aristocrat portable of indeterminate age, and a very old (much older than mine) Singer. All of them work. Around the back and one block south, I find Church Street Antiques, which has lots of antique china and glassware and an interesting Titanic-era seaman's trunk.

It's about time for my table to come up, so I head back to Lunch on Limoges. A hungry and waiting crowd spills from the door, and the hostess is understandably a bit overwhelmed. This frantic atmosphere is part of L. O. L.'s ambiance—probably why they're not open for dinner. I'm sure the staff is exhausted by the time lunch is over. Eventually the hostess finds me a table, and my waitress promptly drops off a basket of their famous fruit-nut-and-banana muffins, served with a sweet, delicious cranberry-pineapple butter. These bite-size delicacies are my reason for coming here. I could easily make a whole meal out of a couple of baskets of these, but then they may not let me come back.

Lunch on Limoges is an interesting place. Lunch tables blend right into the boutique at one end of the large room. The black-and-white checkerboard floor and tall ceilings echo the busy sounds of the open kitchen, which Skip built himself and which occupies one corner of the room. L. O. L. serves what I can best describe as Southern-gourmet fare. The chalkboard menu changes daily, and there are a few regular items. One is the pecan grouper, which I order. Crisp-fried and smothered in lemon, butter, and pecans, this grouper dish is so rich it could pass for dessert. It comes with cauliflower in a cream-pimento sauce and smashed (not quite mashed) potatoes. Raspberry iced tea washes it all down. Then my eyes out-vote my stomach, and I order the towering lemon-meringue pie for dessert, but I'm so stuffed I can manage only about four bites.

It's walk-off-lunch time. I cross Highway 301 and pass the grounds of the county courthouse, where workers are putting up booths for this weekend's Kumquat Festival. Heart's Desire is an antiques shop at the corner of 5th and Church Streets. They have a good selection of antiques and collectible memorabilia, but what fascinates me is their accommodations: a genuine 1912 Sears and Roebuck Catalog bungalow. From 1909 through the 1930s, Sears offered not only the plans but also all the materials (including pre-cut lumber) to build an entire home via mail-order. Their 1926 Catalog of Homes offered everything from a simple, two-bedroom bungalow for $629 to a four-bedroom house with a dining room, den, and porch for $4,909. Looking like a gingerbread house with its decorative roof dormer and beveled roof line, the Heart's Desire house is a superb example of one of Sears' earliest bungalows. (See the Mount Dora chapter in Volume 1 of *Visiting Small-Town Florida* for another Sears and Roebuck mail-order house: The Stanton Childs house, now Odom's Interiors, is a 1928 Sears bungalow.)

A few blocks south on Highway 301 is the Osceola House, built in 1897 and Dade City's oldest still-standing hotel. "It was a boarding house–hotel and popular saloon that catered to the railroad and lumber

Heart's Desire Antiques, a 1912 Sears and Roebuck catalog bungalow in Dade City.

people," current owner Mike tells me. "Right now, we have our antique and gift shop downstairs, and we still rent rooms upstairs. I've been working on returning it to the way it was at the turn of the century. Eventually we'll have a restaurant with the 1890s saloon downstairs, the antiques shop on the second floor, and the third floor will be a bed and breakfast."

From the Osceola House, I head back up to the center of downtown and walk west on Meridian Avenue (State Road 52) to the Azalea House Bed & Breakfast. Grace Bryant, who operates the Azalea House with her daughter Nancy, greets me at the door and offers me the tour. It's an attractive Southern home with a large, wraparound sun porch. Their brochure dates it at 1906. "Actually, we think it was built around 1890 and then relocated to this spot in 1906," Grace explains. "My daughter Nancy spent ten months restoring it before she opened it to the public in 1995." The care that Nancy took is evident; it is a nicely done restoration. There are three rooms, all upstairs. The largest has its own enclosed sleeping porch with twin beds (in addition to the master bedroom's king-size beds).

On my hike back up Meridian Avenue, I stop at the Edwinola Retirement Community in the historic 1912 Edwinola Hotel. This grand, three-story structure was a centerpiece of Dade City social activity in its day. It's easy to picture a Roaring '20s ball taking place in the expansive lobby and dining hall and flowing out onto the broad front verandahs.

In the block just west of Highway 301, on Meridian Avenue, I stop at The Picket Fence, a quaint gift shop in a tiny, bright yellow 1927 cottage. Owner Lori Cunningham says that the house was moved to this location in 1995. Next door at Smith's Antiques & Gifts, I meet part owner Walter Roush, who collects antique license plates. There are quite a few plates up on the wall, some dating back to 1915. "I started collecting automobile license plates a little over thirty years ago when I was in Indiana," Walter tells me. "The earlier East Coast state plates were made from porcelain. They could afford to do that when there weren't that many cars around. Later they started making them from tin." Through his years of collecting, Walter has become an antique license plate connoisseur with an eye for which plates are rare and a good grasp of how valuable they are. His oldest is a 1908 plate from Massachusetts. If you have old automobile license plates, Walter is the man who can tell you all about them.

I'll finish my Dade City afternoon with a visit to the Pioneer Florida Museum on the north edge of town. When it opened in 1961, the museum displayed pioneer-era (1800s to early 1900s) farm implements and equipment that had been donated to the Pasco County Fair. Since then, the museum has expanded considerably, acquiring five pioneer-era buildings and relocating them to the museum grounds: the 1878 Enterprise Methodist Church; a shoe-repair shop built in 1913; the 1896 Trilby, Florida, train depot; a bright red one-room schoolhouse from Lacoochee, Florida, built in 1926; and an 1860's farmhouse. Walking through the farmhouse gives me a sense of what daily life was like in the 1800s. It belonged to John Overstreet, who built it from native heart pine—cut with a steam-operated band saw and hand tools—on his eighty-acre homestead farm near here. As was customary in those days, the kitchen was in a separate room behind the house and was connected to the house by a covered walkway. If a fire started in the kitchen, there was less chance that it would burn down the whole house.

The museum's main building displays locally found pioneer artifacts plus some much older items. One display case features an impressive collection of archaic arrowheads, some of them dating back to 3000-5000 B.C.

Dade City is a terrific small-town escape—particularly for me when I have only half a day, since it's less than fifty minutes from my front door.

DIRECTIONS: Take Highway 301 north from Tampa. Continue north through Zephyrhills.

DON'T MISS: Pioneer Florida Museum

ADDRESSES AND EVENTS: See page 156

CORTEZ

Population: 500 (estimated)

*H*OLLYWOOD DIRECTOR ALFONSO CUARON SEARCHED the entire east coast of the United States for ideal locations to film his modern interpretation of Dickens' *Great Expectations* (1998 release, Twentieth Century Fox). He found what he was looking for at John and Mable Ringling's Venetian Gothic mansion, Cà d' Zan, on Sarasota Bay and at the tiny community of Cortez, just north of Sarasota, on the mainland side of the Intracoastal Waterway. In the movie, Cortez is the boyhood fishing-village home of the central character (Pip in Dickens' original story; Finn in Cuaron's adaptation).

Cortez occupies the western tip of a point of land that juts out into

Anna Maria Sound. I reach it from Bradenton Beach via Highway 684/Cortez Road Bridge. Cuaron wanted a quiet village where commercial fishing was the primary livelihood of its residents. Places such as these are fast becoming a thing of the past in Florida, and Cortez may be one of the last.

Almost everything in Cortez has some relationship to seafood, fishing, or boats. Signs along Cortez Road advertise smoked mullet, fresh shrimp, outboard motor repair, bait, and fishing charters. At a warehouse-size shop with the intriguing name Nautical But Nice, I rummage through shelves of salvaged seagoing hardware-turned-decoration, ship's wheels, portholes, and compasses plus gold doubloons and carved driftwood art. The most fascinating items are three very old, brass diving helmets, sitting high up on a shelf and collecting dust.

Traffic comes to a standstill on Highway 684/Cortez Road when the bridge is up (it frequently is). I turn south on a side street to leave the traffic jam and enter a quiet neighborhood of simple clapboard cottages. Boat docks and fish warehouses line the south shoreline of Cortez. In the mid-1800s, this peninsula was known as Hunter's Point. The locals called the area "The Kitchen" because of the abundance of seafood and shellfish that could be caught in these waters. In 1888, a post office was established here, and the name Cortez was submitted. "Cortez" may be a reference to Spanish explorer Hernando Cortes, who conquered Mexico and the Aztecs for Spain in 1519. However, there is no indication that Cortes ever explored Florida.

The town grew into a small but busy fishing community, with mullet netting, processing, and shipping the primary industry. Much of Cortez' history is defined as before- or after-1921, when a hurricane (prior to when hurricanes were given names) blew in from the Gulf without warning. A storm surge destroyed the docks and sank whole fleets of fishing boats. A large passenger steamship, the *Mistletoe*, went down in the storm. Residents crowded into the town's brick schoolhouse for shelter while their homes washed away. The only building left standing on Cortez' waterfront was the Albion Inn/Hotel.

I am looking for a building that I might recognize as young Finn's house from the movie *Great Expectations*. Cortez isn't too big, and I find it at the south end of 23rd Street West after only ten minutes of searching. The two-story structure is nearly camouflaged by the palmetto scrubs, palm trees, and Australian pines that surround it. A sign over the front entranceway, handpainted on well-weathered driftwood, reads "N. E. Taylor Boatworks." Above it, a newer (but also handpainted) sign proclaims, "Twentieth Century Fox ('Great Expectations') adds history to Cortez, Fla." I'm debating whether or not it would be impolite to knock on the door and ask if I could take some pictures, when a gentleman wearing a fishing cap walks down the outside steps. Alcee Taylor and I trade introductions. He was born in Cortez in 1923 and grew up in this house, built the same year he was born. The upstairs was his family's home (and still is home to Alcee and his wife). The downstairs was his father's business, the Boatworks.

"Sometime around 1908, my father [Neriah Elijah Taylor] moved down [from North Carolina]. His brother had come first, then he followed and brought my mother down," Alcee explains.

I've interrupted Alcee's lunch: He's snacking on a wedge of cheese but doesn't seem to mind the intrusion and leads me in through the side door. "The foundation of this house and the siding was built from driftwood lumber that washed away from down at Longboat Pass during the storm [hurricane] of 1921. My father built boats in here. I've been taking all the old tools and equipment and kind of making it into a museum."

Inside, seventy-five years' worth of woodworking and boat-building equipment—every size and shape of saw, all variety of hand drills, jigs, hardware, and templates—fills what was once a small factory for building 18- to 20-foot pole skiffs and 22- to 26-foot V-hull launches. Back then, two iron rails, used for sliding completed boats down to the water, ran the length of the floor, out the back overhead door, and into the bay.

"In the middle there is where the cradle came up to pull boats out," Alcee explains as we carefully weave our way through his father's shop, around stacks of wood and materials that were used decades ago for constructing boats. He points out items of interest as we pass them. "There's one of the patterns used for building a skiff. And this here is a natural-crook cedar timber." He holds up a hefty tree limb that has grown into an arc. "You had to go out into the mangrove swamps, off Longboat Key, to find pieces of wood with just the right bend in them

*N. E. Taylor Boatworks in Cortez, where Neriah Elijah Taylor began
his boat building business around 1908.*

to make your framing for the boat. They had to all line up, where you
could carry the flare back on each side of the boat. You'd saw them
down the center with the cross-cut saw and have two matching pieces,
one for each side of the keel."

Alcee's two older brothers built boats with his father. Alcee didn't
build them himself, but he did go into the woods and help haul lumber
back. "There were a lot more mosquitoes back then," he recalls. "I've
seen them so thick on the screen window upstairs that you had to beat
the screen to get air to flow through."

In addition to displaying all of N. E. Taylor's boat-building equipment, Alcee has compiled a large collection of old photographs and
newspaper articles. He shows me before- and after-1921 hurricane photos of the docks in Cortez. Then he pulls out a 1932 N. E. Taylor
Boatworks invoice for a completed boat. It reads, "Boat: $350.00.
Lumber: $65.00." They charged two dollars for a "pull-out" to winch the
boat out of the water. He pulls out a receipt from Southern Utilities

Company, dated June, 12, 1925. "That's when we got electricity and lights put in the house."

The centerpiece of Alcee's museum is a 1936 donkey boat. Why is it called a donkey boat? "Back in them days they used tractors, Model Ts, horses, mules, donkeys, whatever, to pull the nets in from the beaches. My dad had bought a motor that he was going to put over there with the winch so he'd have power to pull up [boats] with. Some fishermen got to talking with him—they figured they could mount that motor in a boat, hook it to a truck transmission and a pulley, anchor the boat out in the water, run a rope out, and pull nets with it. That's what they did. It took the place of the donkey, so they called it a donkey boat."

Among Alcee's photographs are recent shots of the *Great Expectations* film crew shooting scenes at his house. "See all these big panels of lights on the scaffoldings? They had so many lights going all around the house one night that folks down at Longboat thought Cortez was on fire." One photograph shows the entire two-story building wrapped in black plastic. Alcee explains, "They wrapped the whole house—trees out in front even—to make it look like nighttime inside. Then they'd make it look like it was raining and lightning." The crew worked at Alcee's house and on the docks nearby for three and half months in 1996. Twentieth Century Fox moved Alcee and his wife, Betty, to a condominium on the beach for the duration of the filming. "We came back over every day to watch the filming. It was quite fascinating. . . ."

I ask Alcee if he's seen a lot of changes in Cortez over the years. "Yeah," he says, then hesitates a moment. "Too many. And not for the good." In 1995, a referendum-voted net ban went into effect. No nets larger than five hundred square feet could be used. It was the most hotly debated item on Florida's November 1994 ballot. It pitted sport fishermen, who claimed that commercial netters were depleting the fish population, against commercial fishermen. The pro-net ban group waged ad campaigns that showed dolphins and turtles snagged in the nets of large offshore netting trawlers. Ironically, these particular operations work far enough offshore to be outside the state's jurisdiction and are therefore not subject to the ban. The smaller, closer-to-shore commercial fishermen were legislated into immediate near-extinction. Obviously, Cortez

The docks at Cortez, many of them rebuilt following the 1921 hurricane.

Alcee Taylor, son of Neriah Elijah Taylor, at N. E. Taylor Boatworks in Cortez.

was and is vehemently anti-net ban. Signs in the front yards and on the bumper stickers on most of the cars proclaim this. Alcee comments on it: "I appreciate all them people who afterwards told me they was misled. And they was. We didn't have the money to put out what we had to say, on the TV and in the magazines and all, like they [the pro-net ban group] did. Yeah, the voters was misled. And communities like Cortez and whole generations of families whose lives have centered around fishing will pay the price."

On living here, Alcee tells me, "I do like Cortez. There are good folks here. You can still get out and walk around whenever and wherever you want to."

On my way out of Cortez I stop at Annie's Bait and Tackle, next to the bridge, for a quick bite. A sign above the bar lauds their smoked mullet spread. "Sorry. We're out," the waitress explains. "Can't get mullet regularly like we used to." I settle for the barbecued pork sandwich and am subtly reminded that things in Cortez may never again be like they used to be.

DIRECTIONS: Go east of Bradenton Beach across Highway 684 Bridge or west of Interstate 75 off Cortez Road exit.

DON'T MISS: N. E. Taylor Boatworks

ADDRESSES AND EVENTS: See page 157

SOUTH REGION

INDIAN
RIVER

Stuart

CHARLOTTE

GLADES

75

LEE

PALM BEACH

Palm
Beach

Fort Myers

95

ESTERO

HENDRY

BROWARD

COLLIER

75

Naples

Fort
Lauderdale

DADE

MONROE

Miami

STILTSVILLE

N

1

NO NAME KEY

1

Key West

BIG PINE KEY

ESTERO

Population: 2,000 (estimated)

*A*T THE CROSSING OF US HIGHWAY 41 and the Estero (Spanish for "estuary") River, I pull into Estero River Outfitters, which rents and sells kayaks and canoes. Inside, I talk to Jeff about paddling the river. "The Estero is spring fed. The main spring is about a mile east of here," he explains. "Then the river winds west from here about four miles until it spills into the bay and then another mile out to Mound Key."

Mound Key was a thriving Calusa Indian village known as Calos when Spanish explorers first ran across it nearly five hundred years ago. The Calusa and their ancestors had populated this region for fifteen hundred years prior to that, but they died out by the mid-1700s from

117

exposure to European diseases from which they had no immunity. Three thirty-foot-high shell mounds rise from Mound Key's center—the only obvious reminders that the Calusa were there.

"The water turns brackish from here west," Jeff continues. "Lots of bass and snook. It's a scenic paddle, particularly where you pass through the Koreshan State Historic Site."

The town of Estero is now a quiet residential community, but one hundred years ago it was the setting for one of the oddest chapters in Florida history. In 1869, Dr. Cyrus Teed, a medical doctor living near Syracuse, New York, experienced what he labeled "an illumination, a vision." Teed had recently become disgruntled with conventional medicine and had begun studying metaphysics. During this illumination, according to Teed, a list of universal truths was revealed to him by an angel. Following that experience, he felt compelled to form an organization based on what he had divined. His initial attempts in New York failed, but in 1886 in Chicago, he generated enough of a following to incorporate his "College of Life." Two years later he opened a communal home there where his followers could reside. Cyrus Teed adopted the name Koresh (which is ancient Hebrew for Cyrus); his organization evolved into the Koreshan Unity, and his doctrine became known as Koreshanity. In 1894, Teed purchased three hundred acres along the Estero River from German immigrant Gustave Damkohler (one of the earliest settlers in what is now Estero) on which to begin building a communal "New Jerusalem." The Koreshans believed in a celibate lifestyle for those who worked full-time in the operation of the commune. Teed counted on outside recruits to grow their numbers.

Teed's beliefs had some basis in Christianity, although he believed that the Bible was written symbolically and required the interpretation of a prophet. Koreshanity mixed theological, sociological, and (supposed) scientific theories into one philosophy. One of his most bizarre beliefs was something called "Cellular Cosmogony," which purported that the surface of the Earth was on the inside of a giant sphere, and that the sun (which revolved and had both a light and a dark side), the planets, and space existed in the center of that sphere. Teed was so intent on convincing the scientific community that this was indeed the case that he staged an experiment to prove it. The Koreshan Unity's "geodetic" staff constructed an enormous accordion-like contraption, which they named "The Rectilineater," to prove their hypothesis. It stretched out from the beach into Estero Bay. No one really seems to understand exactly what it was supposed to measure, but the geodetic staff claimed that it substantiated their theory. They were so confident in their findings that they offered ten thousand dollars to anyone who could disprove them. Apparently no one ever bothered to challenge them.

While the Koreshans certainly had their weird side, they were also very industrious people. They farmed citrus, shipped fruit, operated printing presses, and ran a sawmill, a boat building business, a general store, a bakery, and eventually a restaurant. They even had their own well-known and popular concert band. Although they were a commune, they conducted business and interacted regularly with outsiders. The Koreshan Unity continued to acquire property and in 1904 owned about seventy-five hundred acres.

Cyrus "Koresh" Teed died in 1908, and the Koreshan Unity's population began a slow decline. In 1961, the handful of remaining Koreshans donated the Koreshan Unity property to the State of Florida to become a state historic site. Hedwig Michel was the last president of the Koreshan Unity and the last living Koreshan. She died at age 90 in 1982.

The Koreshan State Historic Site rests on the 305 donated acres on the east side of Highway 41, between Corkscrew Road and the Estero River. Before going there, I stop to visit the Koreshan Unity Foundation headquarters, across Highway 41 from the State Historic Site.

The Koreshan Unity Foundation is a nonprofit organization whose purpose is to preserve the Koreshan's historical heritage. Most importantly, they are the keepers of all the original Koreshan archives. The circular-shaped headquarters building is architecturally striking in a Frank Lloyd Wright-ish kind of way. It triples as the foundation's offices, library, and museum.

Sarah Bergquist, my tour host, tells me, "This building is named for Hedwig Michel. It was designed by architect Martin Gunderson and completed in 1979. The idea for the basic design and shape was Hedwig's. She specified the circular shape to represent her hope for the unending existence of Koreshanity."

Sarah points out that no employees at the foundation are Koreshan.

In other words, they do not believe that we live on the inside of the earth. "Our interest is from a historical preservation standpoint," she explains. "We have all of the Koreshan archives and are currently in the process of transcribing their letters, documents, and publications. Dr. Teed was a particularly prolific writer and an avid reader."

Shelves of books from Teed's personal library fill several walls. A few of the books are so old that no one will even attempt to open them. Pictures cover the rest of the walls—old photographs that document daily Koreshan life and paintings by Douglas Arthur Teed. Douglas Teed was Cyrus Teed's son (who was born, presumably, prior to Dr. Teed's commitment to celibacy) and an accomplished artist who studied in Europe. Interestingly, he chose not to be a Koreshan. The foundation has also collected furniture and artifacts that belonged to the Koreshan Unity, including many items from Dr. Teed's residence, among them his folding Murphy bed. Teed also loved music and encouraged its teaching, and his piano and organ are here on display.

"Dr. Teed's vision was that New Jerusalem (Estero) would be an enormous hub-shaped city, large enough to be home to ten million people. His detailed plan included such far-thinking ideas as underground passageways to carry out refuse, which would then be recycled and returned as compost," Sarah tells me. "He sincerely felt that he was the shepherd to his people. We read that he was a very dynamic and convincing speaker, and that his followers were quite devoted. Of course, the New Jerusalem plan never came to fruition. People who pass through here regularly comment, 'Is it any wonder that they died out? They didn't believe in reproducing!' This is a common misunderstanding. It's true that Dr. Teed advocated celibacy but only for those who worked full-time in the leadership, governing, and operation of the commune. These people lived in separate dormitories, while Koreshans who had families lived in outlying cottages."

Granted, there were some peculiarities about these folks, but unlike most other religious cults and communes, the Koreshans were inclusive. They interacted happily with and were a part of the surrounding communities. They always welcomed outsiders and never condemned others for disagreeing with their doctrine.

My next stop is the Koreshan State Historic Site. Spending the earlier part of the day at the Koreshan Unity Foundation headquarters and museum has given me a much greater appreciation for what I'm seeing. Many of the original buildings have been restored, and the grounds appear much as they did one hundred years ago. Among the restored buildings are Dr. Teed's two-story house (the "Founder's House"), built in 1896 and the oldest standing original-settlement building; the "New Store," built in the early 1920s—a general store, post office, and restaurant that catered to passing traffic on Tamiami Trail (Highway 41); and the "Planetary Court," built in 1904 and painted bright yellow with green trim. This is where the women of the Planetary Chamber, the Koreshan's day-to-day governing council, lived and maintained their offices. Henry Silverfriend, the women's guardian, lived in its roof-top apartment. The building that I find most interesting is the 1905 Arts Hall. This was the Koreshans' social and community center. Now it serves as a museum that features a model of the Rectilineater along with photographs and paintings. One large painting depicts an aerial view of the anticipated New Jerusalem. There is also a globe that demonstrates the theory of Cellular Cosmogony.

Koreshan Unity Foundation headquarters in Estero, where the archives of
Dr. Cyrus Teed, founder of the Koreshan Unity, are kept.

Perhaps Hedwig Michel's wish has come true. While the Koreshans and their beliefs have died out, the remains of their odd world and existence are being preserved by the Koreshan Unity Foundation and the Koreshan State Historic Site.

DIRECTIONS: Take US Highway 41 south of Fort Myers.

DON'T MISS: Koreshan Unity Foundation Museum

ADDRESSES AND EVENTS: See page 157

STILTSVILLE

Population: full-time 0; part-time, anywhere from 1 to 100

*I*N CARL HIAASEN'S 1989 NOVEL SKIN TIGHT, protagonist/ex-State's Attorney investigator/sometimes private eye Mick Stranahan lives in one of a dozen wooden houses perched on stilts out in the middle of Biscayne Bay. The "neighborhood" is called Stiltsville. I thought Hiaasen had dreamed it up until I happened across a *Miami Herald* article about local concern that the National Park Service may be trying to demolish it.

Admittedly, it's a bit of a stretch to suggest that Stiltsville qualifies as a small-town, but I just have to see this place. South Florida pals Doug and Terrie and I commandeer a twenty-one-foot bow-rider from Club

Nautico, next to Monty Trainers Restaurant in Coconut Grove. After twenty minutes idling out of the marina, passing moored yachts worthy of a James Bond movie, we open up the throttle and motor south across Biscayne Bay.

While Doug drives, I try to read the charts, and Terrie scans the horizon with her binoculars. Stiltsville should show up somewhere south of Key Biscayne but well north of Elliott Key. Biscayne National Park stretches from the southern tip of Key Biscayne to the northern tip of Key Largo. It is probably the National Park system's most unusual park, in that 95 percent of its 180,000 acres are underwater. Seven-mile-long Elliott Key is its only substantial piece of dry land. Spectacular coral reefs, brimming with tropical sea life, rest just beneath the surface. Lots of exciting history has taken place in these waters. Villainous pirates, including the infamous Black Cesar, who lived on Elliott Key for a while, frequented these waters in the 1700s. The shallow reefs have been a graveyard for ships as far back as history records. In 1942, a German submarine sank a tanker, killing fourteen men, just offshore from Key Biscayne.

Miami Springs Powerboat Club in Stiltsville, a community of stilt houses
built on the shallow flats of Biscayne bay.

Biscayne National Park was created in 1980, forty years after the first stilt houses went up in the shallow flats of Biscayne Bay. Stiltsville's first "homesteader" was a fisherman named "Crawfish" Eddie Walker. Sometime in the mid-1930s, Crawfish Eddie staked his claim on an abandoned run-aground barge. He built a bait-and-beer shack on one end and went into business, selling to passing fishermen. In 1939, another Eddie—Turner this time—built a bar and restaurant on pilings not far from Crawfish Eddie's called the Quarterdeck Club.

This was the beginning of Stiltsville's wild era. Rumors of unruly parties and debauchery spread. After *Life* magazine ran an article about the Quarterdeck Club in 1941, word was out. Not everybody was happy about it. Some of the new and well-to-do residents of Key Biscayne were displeased about the near-offshore activity. Those protests not withstanding, people began to build weekend fishing cabins on stilts out in the bay in the mid-1940s. The Quarterdeck Club burned in the early 1950s, but others took its place. Harry "Pierre" Churchville opened the Biscayne Bay Bikini Club in 1962 on a grounded one-hundred-fifty-foot yacht. Three years later, Florida State Beverage agents shut it down for operating without a liquor license. Stiltsville mellowed a bit after that.

Up until 1969, the stilt houses stood free of property taxes or rent. That year the State of Florida began charging the "squatters" a property lease fee. Stiltsville had as many as twenty houses in the 1970s. Hurricanes took their toll on some. By the 1980s, the houses numbered in the mid-teens. After Hurricane Andrew blew through in August 1992, only seven were left standing. None can be rebuilt because of National Park restrictions on building or rebuilding residential structures. In fact, those seven remaining houses are scheduled to be destroyed by July 1999, despite the fact that Stiltsville's existence predates the creation of Biscayne National Park by four decades.

I'm not having much luck reading the charts, so I pass them on to Doug. Terrie takes the wheel, and I take her binoculars. Before long, I spot what looks like a shimmering mirage of Chinese pagodas resting on the Atlantic Ocean's horizon a good five miles out. It can only be Stiltsville. Biscayne Bay is very shallow—sometimes less than five feet deep—so we are very careful to follow the channels designated on our chart. We travel further south then turn back up northeast. The first house we come to sits on substantial concrete piers. Boat docks, with several fishing boats tied up, extend from two sides. A water slide sits at the end of one. The entire back wall of the house has an elaborate underwater wildlife mural painted on it. This is the Miami Springs Powerboat Club, and a few of its members are here today. People are fishing off one of the docks. Kids are splashing into the Atlantic off the slide. The rest of the houses are just north, scattered out across the channel from Bill Baggs State Park and the Cape Florida Lighthouse on Key Biscayne's southern tip. They look sturdy and well maintained, all with concrete pilings and some with fresh paint. Beach towels drying on a porch railing indicate that only one other house has occupants today. Obviously, the people who come here these days are trying to get away from all the noise of the big city, not to create any. Their spider-legged domiciles sit in stark contrast to the towering backdrop of downtown Miami.

The National Park Service contends that their first priority is to protect the natural resources within their boundaries. Legitimately, they sight concerns about motorboats damaging the shallow reefs and sea grass beds, sewage removal, and post-storm clean-up. Stilt house owners have formed a group called Save Our Stiltsville and are working on plans to address those concerns. They are also working on obtaining historical status for Stiltsville: That may be its best hope for salvation.

DIRECTIONS: Go due south of Cape Florida and Key Biscayne.

DON'T MISS: Stiltsville (I hope it won't be gone by the time you read this.)

ADDRESSES AND EVENTS: See page 157

BIG PINE KEY
AND
NO NAME KEY

Population: 6,000 (estimated)

*B*IG PINE KEY, THE LARGEST ISLAND IN THE LOWER KEYS, could be Florida's answer to the Galapagos Islands. Along with its northwest appendage, No Name Key, it is home to a number of rare and endangered birds, reptiles, and mammals—including the seldom-sighted, short-eared Lower Keys marsh rabbit (rumored to actually swim between the islands occasionally). Big Pine Key's best-known and most-endangered inhabitant is the petite Key, or "toy," deer. Key deer are the smallest race of North American deer and are endemic to the Lower Keys; nearly the entire population is found on Big Pine and No Name Keys. A typical adult weighs between forty and seventy pounds and

The architecturally eclectic Barnacle Bed & Breakfast on Big Pine Key,
designed and built by Steven "Woody" Cornell in 1976.

stands less than two and half feet tall at the shoulder. Disproportionately large ears and brown eyes add considerably to their "cuteness" quotient. Unfortunately, their adorableness may be one of the factors contributing to their demise.

Commercial development did not take place on Big Pine Key (except for a little joint called the No Name Pub) until the late 1960s, but there have been small settlements here and on No Name Key for over a hundred years. Some of the people who lived here in the mid-1800s were fishermen and spongers, but most were here to harvest buttonwood trees (found in the lower and wetter areas of the island) for charcoal.

Just thirty-five miles south, Key West, the most populous city in Florida in the mid-1800s and the richest per capita, was experiencing its Golden Era. Big Pine Key charcoal was much in demand as a fuel source. Early (1500s) Spanish explorers had called Key West "Cayo Hueso," which means "Island of Bones," presumably because they found piles of bones left there from some long-ago Calusa Indian battle. A couple of centuries later, the moniker was still appropriate, considering that Key West's biggest money crop in the 1800s was the remains (or bones, if you will) of ships smashed on the surrounding reefs. This perfectly legal industry was called "wrecking," and brave Key Westers were making a mint salvaging the cargoes of wrecked ships. Wrecking created both an industrial boom and a population boom in Key West, and that kept Big Pine Key's charcoal industry burning. But nothing lasts forever.

At the end of the nineteenth century, with the construction of light-houses in the Lower Keys to warn ships away from reefs, the wrecking industry died a quick death. Big Pine Key's buttonwood charcoal business, and the settlements that had resulted from it, soon followed suit.

In 1905, Henry Flagler started building his Overseas Railroad and began connecting the dots of the Keys. It rolled across Big Pine Key around 1909 or 1910 and finished in Key West in 1912. The Labor Day Hurricane of 1935—the largest ever to strike Florida—brought an end to the Overseas Railroad when it ripped across the Upper Keys, blasting an entire train sent by Flagler to rescue road workers on Islamorada right off the tracks. (See the Tavernier and Islamorada sections of *Visiting Small-Town Florida*, Volume 1).

By 1938, the Overseas Highway had been paved to Key West, reusing many of Flagler's railway bridges, but Big Pine Key and No Name Key were largely unaffected. Their few inhabitants were mostly fishermen or rumrunners left over from the Prohibition era and seeking anonymity.

In 1957, the U. S. Fish and Wildlife Service established the National Key Deer Refuge on Big Pine and No Name Keys. Hunters had decimated the Key deer population: There were fewer than fifty deer in 1949. First refuge manager and local hero Jack Watson fought vehemently for their survival and is credited with saving them, almost single-handedly, from extinction. He battled poachers like the sheriff in a wild West town, sometimes resorting to sinking their boats and torching their pick-up trucks. Watson retired in 1975, and three years later the Key deer reached its population peak of four hundred. Sadly, their numbers have been on the decline since then. Loss of habitat, automobile strikes, and unusually low birth rates are the three reasons most often cited.

- **Loss of habitat:** The refuge is carved up into numerous sections separated by roads, residential neighborhoods, and commercial development, resulting in loss of habitat for the Key deer.

- **Automobile strikes:** Of the 125 Key deer that died in 1997, 84 were killed by automobiles. Hand-feeding exacerbates the problem. These little guys are so cute that people get out of their cars to feed them. The deer are quick learners, and before long they start running out to cars—and invariably get hit.

- **Low birth rate:** Bill Milling, a volunteer at the Key Deer Refuge office, tells me, "Key deer typically have single births. Multiple births occur only about fifteen percent of the time. Compare that to standard deer, who have multiple births about seventy percent of the time. Currently there are fewer than three hundred Key deer left. We've been averaging forty-five births a year, but with an annual death rate of twice that . . . well, you can do the math."

Publicizing the National Key Deer Refuge is a double-edged sword: the potential for more traffic weighed against the value of an increased awareness of the Key deer's plight. Every person I spoke to in the community said something to me about driving slowly and carefully (whether I asked about it or not). The local police do their part. They write speeding tickets for just one mile per hour over the limit, which is thirty-five miles per hour almost everywhere on the islands.

Big Pine Key is decidedly quieter and more leisurely than its famous neighbor to the south. I am staying for a night at the Barnacle Bed and Breakfast, where leisure has been refined to an art form. Overgrown Long Beach Road dead-ends a short ways past it, so there is no traffic. A simple limestone wall marks the entrance. The Barnacle is an architectural enigma. Its style doesn't fall neatly into any conventional category. Modern, eclectic, nautical, tropical—there are no right angles. Its pipe railings, archways, and generous open-air balcony remind me, more than anything else, of an ocean liner, albeit with an exterior painted in varying shades of earth-tones reminiscent of the 1970s. From the top-floor sunrise-watching deck (the ocean liner's bow), guests can scan the Atlantic's vivid turquoise water for rolling dolphin or maybe a jumping manta ray.

My room, a downstairs "ocean room" (done in shades of pastel sea green and plum), opens directly onto the beach. Multicolored hexagonal tiles cover the floor. Creative use of space for the bathroom, the kitchenette, and shelving reminds me of a state room on the Queen Elizabeth. Again, the walls are skewed at odd angles, and the floor plan is a series of triangles. My bed sits in its own little alcove that faces the ocean through sliding glass doors.

Original owner Steven "Woody" Cornell designed and built the Barnacle in 1976. Dive operators Tim and Jane Marquis bought it from Woody in 1994. "We didn't see any reason to change much of anything that Woody had built," Jane explains in her casual Louisiana accent. "I don't know how Woody came up with the design for this place, but it is definitely an original. Tim and I had been coming down here for years before we bought this place. We love it—it's quiet, laid-back, not rush-rush. We've been in the scuba diving trip business for over twenty years, and buying the Barnacle turned out to be the perfect complement. We can combine a stay here with customized dive packages—out to Looe Key or wherever the customer wants to go—or with fishing trips. We also own five boats. Business is mostly through word of mouth and lately through our Internet web site."

If Tim and Jane's house is an ocean liner, then their beach is the tropical port of call. Five steps outside my room, coconut palms with hammocks strung between them line the shore. More hammocks swing in the breeze under a thatched-roof hut. Tim and Jane offer all kinds of exploration amenities for their guests—kayaks, canoes, sailboats, fishing trips, dive trips—but I choose an early afternoon nap in a hammock before heading over to the Blue Hole.

Back in the 1930s, road construction crews mined the hard oolitic limestone that makes up Big Pine Key. They extracted most of what they needed from one quarry near the center of the island, a place now called the Blue Hole. It's one of the few spots in all the Lower Keys where a substantial amount of fresh rainwater collects, and it is a crucial source of drinking water for the island's wildlife, particularly the Key deer. Highway 940, also called Key Deer Boulevard, cuts a northern path through hardwood hammocks and pinelands, bisecting the largest of the designated Key Deer Refuge areas. The Blue Hole is just off 940 on the left, a mile and a quarter from Highway 1. It is mid-afternoon. The sun is still high and it's hot, so I'm not expecting to see any wildlife.

The Blue Hole is a big football-shaped pond. Even now, fifty years after it was dug, its sharp rock edge reveals that it was manmade. I follow a trail around the south side and then stop at an "overlook." Two soft-shell turtles gaze up at me from just beneath the surface. A school of orange carp (giant goldfish) glides between them. What appears to be a piece of driftwood floats about fifty yards out. Then I notice that the driftwood is leaving a wake behind it. As it gets closer, I recognize the telltale eyes and lumpy snout just breaking the surface. Eight feet behind the snout I can see the tip of a tail, swishing back and forth in slow motion. It's a gator looking for a late lunch!

A short loop trail leads into the hammock from the back side of the Blue Hole. I am impressed at how determined the plant life is around here. Buttonwood, palmetto, slash pines (for which Big Pine Key was named), and gumbo-limbo trees grow right out of the rock with virtually no topsoil. A variety of orchids and air plants use both living and fallen trees as hosts. Halfway around the loop, I run into a group of pith-helmeted, khaki-vested bird watchers from New Jersey. They all have at least two pairs of binoculars and one camera strapped around their necks. They are in bird-watching heaven. "We have seen great white herons, red egrets—we even saw a white-crowned pigeon!" one of them tells me with great excitement. Then he stops talking and tilts his head to one side. I can hear a faint cawing in the distance. "That's an osprey calling its mate," he whispers. As if on cue, an osprey sails across the sky directly overhead. Twenty seconds later, a second osprey follows in its wake. The bird watcher looks at me with a knowing grin.

I have yet to see a Key deer. It's probably too early. The last couple of hours before sunset are the best for spotting them. With an hour to spare, I decide to check out a little joint that one of my readers (whom I met at a *Visiting Small-Town Florida* book signing) insisted I not miss if

I came to Big Pine Key. The No Name Pub sits just around the bend on Wilder Road and just before the bridge over to No Name Key. If it had not been clearly described to me, I would have driven right by without noticing it.

Built in 1936, the No Name Pub was originally a Cuban trading post and general store. It was also reputed to have been a smuggler's hang-out/hideout and a brothel. It has been a bar and restaurant since the mid-1970s, the oldest on the island. Mangroves and cactus half conceal the clapboard building, but a hand-painted sign nailed to a palm tree tells you it's there. Inside, the No Name Pub upholds the Keys' dive bar-decor tradition of stapling signed and dated dollar bills all over the walls and ceiling. Patrons have also carved their initials in the bar, which was built using salvaged scrap from the old wooden No Name Key bridge (now replaced with a sturdier concrete crossing). I'm starting to get hungry, and I notice that every table has a pizza on it. I take the hint and order a medium with onions and mushrooms. It's delicious!

My waitress tells me I'm sure to see Key deer over on No Name Key, and she reminds me to please drive very slowly. Most of No Name Key is designated refuge. No public utilities run to the island. The few hous-es that are here still collect rainwater in cisterns and have generators for power. Unfortunately, I hear that may be changing soon.

Just on the other side of the bridge, I sight my first Key deer, a doe about the size of a springer spaniel. She stops for a moment to scratch one of her oversize ears with a hind hoof, then stares directly into my eyes for a few seconds before trotting off into the woods. Her collar tag identifies her as number 58, and I am reminded again of how few of these graceful animals are left. Further up the road, I watch from a dis-tance as four deer cross in swift hops that seem to defy gravity. Once in the woods, they vanish like a mirage.

The next morning, in the Barnacle's alfresco second-floor central area (I'll call it the lobby, for lack of a better name), Jane serves a full break-fast to her ten guests. We feast on blueberry pancakes, sausages, fresh-cut fruit, and fresh orange juice as we enjoy the feel and smell of the salt breeze. I may be back in that hammock before noon.

DIRECTIONS: Go thirty-five miles north of Key West on Highway A1A.

DON'T MISS: Key deer (But please don't feed them, and do drive slowly!)

ADDRESSES AND EVENTS: See page 158

THREE QUIET BEACHES

Pensacola

BAY

Panama City

MEXICO BEACH

Tallahassee

Lake City

Jacksonville

Saint
Augustine

Gainesville

FLAGLER
FLAGLER
BEACH

Daytona Beach

Ocala

Orlando

Cocoa Beach

Kissimmee

Melbourne

Clearwater

Tampa

St. Petersburg

Bradenton

Fort
Pierce

Sarasota

Stuart

SARASOTA

MANASOTA KEY BEACH

N

Fort Myers

Palm
Beach

Naples

Fort
Lauderdale

Miami

Key West

MANASOTA KEY BEACH, FLAGLER BEACH, AND MEXICO BEACH

Population: Manasota Key Beach 1,000 (estimated);
Flagler Beach 3,820; Mexico Beach 992

*I*N VISITING SMALL-TOWN FLORIDA, VOLUME 1, I sang the praises of Anna Maria, because it had managed to "retain its quiet beach-town flavor." Likewise for St. George Island, Seaside, Boca Grande, and, else-where in this book, Fernandina Beach.

Beach property is the most valuable in Florida. Inevitably, developers try to cram as many sellable living units into as little space as possible. There's really nowhere to go but skyward. The beach ends up with these towering monstrosities that not only mar the scenery and the view but also create bumper-to-bumper traffic (on what is usually a two-lane road) and mobs on the beach. Quiet, private? Forget it. Secluded? Not a chance.

Here are three more quiet little beach towns that haven't been ravaged by over-development (yet). One is on the southwest coast, one the northeast coast, and one in the Panhandle. Nothing of great historical significance happened in any of them. There are no major tourist attractions nearby. They're just nice little beach towns. And you won't have to take out a second mortgage to stay at one of these for a week.

Manasota Key Beach probably gets passed up because it's not easily reached from any major thoroughfare. Interstate 75 steers inland just before it reaches Venice, and Manasota Key is six miles south of Venice. Friends Dean and Carol Howard clued me in to it. They have been coming here for several years, and their favorite restaurant is the Lock and Key at Manasota Key's south end. For dinner one evening, I order crab cakes and grouper fingers (their specialty). Both dishes are excellent. The grouper is caught-that-morning fresh and crispy-fried. Dean orders the prime rib. It is huge and could only have come from a brontosaurus. It hangs over both ends of its Thanksgiving turkey-size platter. Dean tells me it's delicious, but he's convinced he's on "Candid Camera."

Flagler Beach, incorporated in 1925, is roughly halfway between Daytona and St. Augustine on Highway A1A. Its claim to fame is that Charles Lindbergh had to make a forced landing here in 1930, three years after his historic solo crossing of the Atlantic Ocean, and stayed for a few days while his plane was repaired. The nice thing about Flagler is the unobstructed view of the beach from the highway. Motels, shops, and eateries are across the road on the west side of A1A. Don't miss Bill Stead's mural of manatees and tropical fish painted on a retaining wall at South Eighth Street and A1A.

Gazebo at the Driftwood Inn on quiet Mexico Beach.

Mexico Beach is the first real mainland beach that you come to when traveling west on Highway 98 in the Panhandle. Houses sit on a bluff and, across the highway and over sea oats, overlook a wide beach and the emerald Gulf. Mexico Beach was developed in the 1950s and still feels like a beach town from that era. The Driftwood Inn is a quaint beach hotel at the west end of town. The original was built in the early 1950s. In 1975, Tom and Peggy Wood bought it. After a fire destroyed the main building in 1994, the Woods decided to rebuild in an architectural style that mirrored the original. Their lobby doubles as an antique store, and their bright red tin roof and white decorative railings remind me of Seaside. Recently, they've added some separate single and duplex bungalows. Antique furniture, wood floors, and raised ceilings in some units add to the Driftwood's beach-Victorian atmosphere.

DIRECTIONS: **Manasota Key Beach:** Take Highway 775A south from Englewood and cross Beach Road Causeway to Manasota Key Beach.
Flagler Beach: On Highway A1A, go twenty miles north of Daytona Beach to Flagler Beach.
Mexico Beach: On Highway 98, go twelve miles northwest of Port St. Joe to Mexico Beach.

DON'T MISS: Your afternoon nap

ADDRESSES AND EVENTS: See page 158

NOTES ON NEW URBANISM

O F COURSE, THIS BOOK IS ABOUT VISITING small towns and not about moving to them, but it's difficult to talk about small towns today without commenting on the rapidly growing development concept called New Urbanism.

What is New Urbanism? Sometimes called Neo-traditional Town Planning or Traditional Neighborhood Design, New Urbanism is a community design concept that attempts to maximize the interaction of neighbors, to minimize automobile use, and to place a town's (or neighborhood's) living quarters within walking distance of its commercial center. "New" is somewhat of a misnomer. The concept is based largely on old ideas and a return to pre–World War II (read: pre–suburban sprawl) style neighborhoods and towns.

One of the original and best examples of a New Urbanism community is Seaside, Florida (see *Visiting Small-Town Florida*, Volume 1). Seaside was the vision of Robert Davis, who wanted to build a small beach town from scratch that reminded him of those in which he spent his childhood summers in the 1950s. Davis went to husband-and-wife architects Andres Duany and Elizabeth Plater-Zyberk at Arquitectonica in Miami to help plan the layout of Seaside and to draw up the town's building code. In *Visiting Small-Town Florida*, Volume 1, I described Seaside as an ". . . eighty-acre town of all wood-framed, tin-roofed, screen-porched Florida beach cottages in every color the folks at Crayola ever imagined."

The first Seaside houses went up in 1982. Since then, Duany and

141

Plater-Zyberk have been considered the "mom and dad" of the New Urbanism movement. It caught on so well that a contingent of enthusiastic architects and town planners formed a group in 1993 called the Congress for the New Urbanism to promote the concept. The basic ingredients of New Urbanism are as follows:

- High-density housing on narrow lots, with front porches, small picket-fenced front yards, and sidewalks—all to encourage getting to know your neighbors.

- A whole-community plan with a central town square or main street that serves as a commerce and cultural center within walking distance of the extremities of the town or neighborhood.

The two Florida New-Urb towns most often discussed are Seaside (in the Panhandle) and Disney's Celebration (in Kissimmee). The first (and second, and third, and fourth) time I saw Seaside, I was enchanted. For me, Seaside's appeal stems from three things:

- Its charming architecture (with no two houses even remotely alike) that reflects so well the character of the region.

- Its location (on County Road 30A—off the main thoroughfares and as far away from large population centers as it can be).

- Its all non-chain, individually-owned and -run shops and restaurants: The Modica family owns the Modica Market; Dave Rauschkolb and Scott Witcoski own Bud and Alley's Restaurant; Bob and Linda White own Seadog Books.

The first time I saw Celebration, I was disappointed. Here's my impression of Celebration:

- The home architecture is bland, duplicative (many of the houses are choose-from-one-of-our-standard-floor-plans types), and has no connection to the character of the region. It is devoid of personality and could just as easily be sitting in the middle of Kansas as in the middle of Florida. The downtown feels like a movie set. I was certain that if I looked behind the store fronts, I would find that they were just that—fronts propped up by two-by-fours. I know people in Orlando who refer to Celebration as "Stepford."

• The choice of location is horrendous and flies in the face of everything that is good about small towns. Celebration is wedged between Interstate 4 (at perhaps the busiest stretch of interstate in Florida) and the town of Kissimmee, (in my opinion) the tackiest, most embarrassing piece of real estate in the state. As I drove out of Celebration's main entrance/exit, the first things I saw were a Watermania and a giant flashing sign for the World's Largest Gift Shop.

• Rather than appearing to be the creation of someone with vision, Celebration has "corporate design committee" painted all over it. Many of the businesses are chains that I could find at any big-city mall: The coffee shop is a Barnies; the grocery store is a Goodings (a large Orlando-based chain); the theater is an AMC.

Obviously, I think the Celebration guys missed the point. Great small towns are those that flourish apart from massive population centers and all the baggage that accompanies them—traffic, crowds, crime, and the sense of being just another ant in a giant ant farm. Small-town atmosphere cannot be created instantly; it has to evolve. A place's history and the generations of people who have lived there are what shape a small town's personality, not some corporate developer's marketing staff. Perhaps the most important difference between Seaside and Celebration is that Seaside is the result of one man's dream, and its theme is based on his vision. Celebration was built by committee, and it shows.

So, do I like New Urbanism? In some instances, it's good; in others, it's not. When it ignores local culture, history, and character, I consider it an abomination. When it embraces these elements, I applaud it. I still think the best New-Urb project is to revitalize an Old Urb. Plenty of existing small towns in Florida have good basic street plans that mirror what New Urbanism stands for. The best examples of New Urbanism philosophy already working can be found in some of Florida's oldest small towns: Apalachicola, Fernandina, Mt. Dora. Developers would do best to take a look at these before building an instant, just-add-water town.

Postscript:

Unfortunately, the last time I visited Seaside, I noticed an unsettling trend. Scores of (bad) imitators are popping up all around it. County Road 30A is changing from "Off the beaten path" to "It is the beaten path." The resulting traffic jams and overcrowding could destroy the area's charm.

NOTES ON HISTORY

THREE YEARS OF RESEARCH IN WRITING two *Visiting Small-Town Florida* books have given me a keen understanding of the importance of history and its value to society. We always hear about "reading, writing, and arithmetic," but I remember my elementary school classes being "reading, writing, arithmetic, and history."

History—it's nothing but a collection of remembrances of things that have happened. Why should history be important enough to include with these other primary components of education? After some thought, I believe the reasons narrow down to three main ones:

- History is our best guide for how we should conduct ourselves in the future. We learn by studying the mistakes of the past and by making sure we don't repeat them. Perhaps more importantly, we learn by studying the people who have done the right things in history.

- History answers the universal questions we all ask: Who are we? Where are we from? Who are our ancestors? What things did they do, and what events took place that eventually brought us to the point where we are today? When I say 'Who are we?,' I mean it in both the broadest societal sense and the narrowest individual sense. How my grandparents came to Florida is just as important to me as who the first explorers were to set foot in Florida. Both are a part of my heritage.

• This reason is more ethereal, more difficult to describe. A throw back to the 1960s might call this the more "cosmic" answer. History is important because of the magic that we feel when we stand in the same spot where an event took place a long time ago, an event so significant that it altered the direction of things to come and changed how generations of people would live. I feel something magic when I stand in one of those spots, but I can feel it only if I know the history of what took place there. It's as if the spirit of that past event or of the people who participated in that event is still there—as long as we can know, understand, and appreciate what happened.

I've come to realize that, in a way, I'm a part of this chain of historical information, and therefore I have a responsibility to seek out the most accurate sources. Ideally, history would be an exact science, but unfortunately it is largely dependent on people's recollections. Invariably, reports get some coloration, slant, or interpretation according to the reporter's feelings about the situation. And, naturally, the more layers—third-, fourth-, fifth-hand information—and the more versions, interpretations, and embellishments, the less accurate the information. Do these things change history? Probably. Usually we can get the gist of what happened, but in the course of my research I commonly find discrepancies, even between reports from sources considered to be reliable. It usually concerns something simple, such as a date or the source for the name of a town or the names of a town's first settlers. Sometimes it isn't clear which version is the most accurate, and in those cases all I can do is explain that there are conflicting versions and give both.

Some of my most reliable sources are local historical societies. Historical societies are good at gathering first-hand knowledge. I know that some small towns' historical societies have gone to great lengths to gather information from as close to the original source as possible, collecting letters and memoirs from local residents and even videotaping conversations with them.

If your town has a historical society, please support it, not just with money (although that certainly helps) but with the donation of your time: conducting research and interviews, compiling historical documents, restoring historical sites and structures—in short, saving your heritage. Future generations will appreciate it.

Happy exploring!

APPENDIX
Addresses and Events

NORTH REGION

MILTON AND BAGDAD

Arcadia Mill Site Museum
5701 Mill Pond Road
Milton, Florida 32583
(850) 626-4433

Bagdad Village Preservation
   Association Museum
4512 Church Street
Bagdad, Florida 32530
(850) 623-5390

The Cutting Board Restaurant
5365 Stewart Street
Milton, Florida 32570
(850) 623-2929

Old Mill House Gallery
4621 Forsyth Street
Bagdad, Florida 32530
(850) 623-0783

Santa Rosa Chamber of Commerce
5247 Stewart Street
Milton, Florida 32570-4737
(850) 623-2339

Santa Rosa Historical Society
Caroline Street
Milton, Florida 32570
(850) 623-4998

West Florida Railroad Museum
206 Henry Street
Milton, Florida 32570
(850) 623-3645

Events:
Scratch Ankle Festival: second or third weekend in March, (850) 983-4998

Depot Days: second weekend in November, (850) 623-4998

TWO EGG

Lawrence Grocery
3972 Wintergreen Road
Two Egg/Greenwood, Florida 32443

QUINCY

The Allison House Inn
215 North Madison Street
Quincy, Florida 32351
(850) 875-2511

Gadsden Carriage House Restaurant
104 East Washington Street
Quincy, Florida 32351
(850) 875-4660

Gadsden County Chamber of
Commerce
P. O. Box 389
221 North Madison
Quincy, Florida 32351
(850) 627-9231

McFarlin House Bed & Breakfast
Inn
305 East King Street
Quincy, Florida 32351
(850) 875-2526

Events:
Quincy Days: first weekend in October, (850) 627-9231

Gadsden County Art Festival: each weekend from October through December, (850) 627-9231

HAVANA

Antiques & Accents
213 First Street NW
Havana, Florida 32333
(850) 539-0073

The Cannery
115 East Eighth Avenue
Havana, Florida 32333
(850) 539-3800

Dolly's Expresso Cafe
206 First Street NW
Havana, Florida 32333
(850) 539-6716

Florida Art Center & Gallery
208 First Street NW
Havana, Florida 32333
(850) 539-1770

Gaver's Bed and Breakfast
301 East Sixth Avenue
Havana, Florida 32333
(850) 539-5611

H & H Antiques
302 North Main Street
Havana, Florida 32333
(850) 539-6886

The Happy Hippo
123 East Seventh Avenue
Havana, Florida 32333
(850) 539-5370

Historical Bookshelf Ltd.
104 East Seventh Avenue
Havana, Florida 32333
(850) 539-5040

Kudzu Plantation
102 East Seventh Avenue
Havana, Florida 32333
(850) 539-0877

Little River General Store & Trading
   Company
308 North Main Street
Havana, Florida 32333
(850) 539-6900

McLauchlin House
201 South Seventh Avenue
Havana, Florida 32333
(850) 539-0901

Nicholson Farmhouse Restaurant
State Road 12
Havana, Florida 32333
(850) 539-5931

The Planter's Exchange
204 Second Street NW
Havana, Florida 32333
(850) 539-6364

Sherrill McNeece Photographic Art
Route 1, Box 3317
Havana, Florida 32333
(850) 539-6737

Twin Willows Cafe
211 First Street NW
Havana, Florida 32333
(850) 539-9111

Events:
   Havana Music Fest: first weekend
   in March, (850) 627-9231

   Old Time Havana Days Festival:
   second weekend in May, (850)
   627-9231

   Pepper Festival: last weekend in
   July, (850) 627-9231

   Florida Art Center National 100
   Art Show: third weekend in
   September, (805) 539-1770

WAKULLA SPRINGS

Edward Ball Wakulla Springs State
   Park and Lodge
550 Wakulla Park Drive
Wakulla Springs, Florida 32305
Lodge (850) 224-5950
Park (850) 922-3632

Museum of Florida History
R. A. Gray Building
500 South Bronough Street
Tallahassee, Florida 32399-0250

ST. MARKS

Posey's Oyster Bar
P. O. Box 112
St. Marks, Florida 32355
(850) 925-6172

St. Marks National Wildlife Refuge
P. O. Box 68
St. Marks, Florida 32355
(850) 925-6121

Sweet Magnolia Bed and Breakfast
803 Port Leon Drive
St. Marks, Florida 32355

Tallahassee-to-St. Marks Historic
   Trail
1022 DeSoto Park Drive
Tallahassee, Florida 32301-4555
(904) 922-6007

JASPER

H & F Restaurant
Hatley Street and 2nd Avenue
Jasper, Florida 32052
(904) 792-3074

ADAMS BEACH, DEKLE BEACH, AND
KEATON BEACH

Keaton Beach Hot Dog Stand
21239 Keaton Beach Drive
Keaton Beach, Florida 32347
(850) 578-2675

Taylor County Chamber of
   Commerce
P. O. Box 892
Perry, Florida 32348
(850) 584-5366

FERNANDINA

The Addison House
614 Ash Street
Fernandina Beach, Florida 32034
(904) 277-1604
(800) 943-1604

Amelia Island/Fernandina Beach
   Chamber of Commerce
The Depot, Centre Street
P. O. Box 472
Fernandina Beach, Florida 32035
(904) 261-3248
(800) 2-AMELIA

Amelia Island Gourmet Coffee
   Company
3 North Fourth Street
Fernandina Beach, Florida 32034
(904) 321-2111

Amelia Island Museum of History
233 South 3rd Street
Fernandina Beach, Florida 32034
(904) 261-7378

The Bailey House
28 South Seventh Street
Fernandina Beach, Florida 32034
(904) 261-5390
(800) 251-5390

The Beech Street Grill
801 Beech Street
Fernandina Beach, Florida 32034
(904) 277-3662

The Book Loft
214 Centre Street
Fernandina Beach, Florida 32034
(904) 261-8991

Celtic Charm
306 Centre Street
Fernandina Beach, Florida 32034
(904) 277-8009

Centre Street Treasures
216 Centre Street
Fernandina Beach, Florida 32034
(904) 277-6626

Crab Trap Restaurant
31 North Second Street
Fernandina Beach, Florida 32034
(904) 261-4749

The Cross-Eyed Bear
201 Centre Street
Fernandina Beach, Florida 32034
(904) 261-7924

Designs On . . . Gallery
11 North Third Street
Fernandina Beach, Florida 32034
(904) 277-4104

Elizabeth Pointe Lodge
98 South Fletcher Avenue
Amelia Island, Florida 32034
(904) 277-4851

The Fairbanks House
227 South Seventh Street
Fernandina Beach, Florida 32034
(904) 277-0500
(800) 261-4838

Florida House Inn
20 & 22 South Third Street
Fernandina Beach, Florida 32034
(904) 261-3300

Fort Clinch State Park
2601 Atlantic Avenue
Fernandina Beach, Florida 32034
(904) 277-7174

H2O Outfitters/Kayak Tours
1925 South 14th Street
Fernandina Beach, Florida 32034
(904) 321-0697

Island Aerial Tours
1600 Airport Road
Fernandina Beach, Florida 32034
(904) 321-0904

Le Clos Restaurant
20 South Second Street
Fernandina Beach, Florida 32034
(904) 261-8100

The Main Squeeze Juice Bar
105 South Third Street
Fernandina Beach, Florida 32034
(904) 277-3003

The Marina Restaurant
101 Centre Street
Fernandina Beach, Florida 32034
(904) 261-5310

Palace Saloon
117 Centre Street
Fernandina Beach, Florida 32034
(904) 261-6320

A Touch of England
316B Centre Street
Fernandina Beach, Florida 32034
(904) 261-8008

The Unusual Shop
308 Centre Street
Fernandina Beach, Florida 32034
(904) 277-9664

Waterwheel Art Enterprises
316A Centre Street
Fernandina Beach, Florida 32034
(904) 277-7908

Events:
St. Patrick's Day Parade and
Celebration: March 15, (904)
277-4006

Shrimp Festival: second weekend
in May, (904) 261-0203

Heritage Classic Car Celebration:
third weekend in October, (904)
277-0717

CRESCENT CITY

Crescent City Chamber of
Commerce
115 North Summit Street
Crescent City, Florida 32112
(904) 698-1657

Native Traditions Gallery
10 Summit Street
Crescent City, Florida 32112
(904) 698-4433

Sprague House Inn and Restaurant
125 Central Avenue
Crescent City, Florida 32112
(904) 698-2430

Total Interiors Gifts and Antiques
338 Central Avenue
Crescent City, Florida 32112
(904) 698-3420

Events:
St. John's River Catfish Festival:
first Saturday in April, (904)
698-1657

CENTRAL REGION

MCINTOSH

Ft. McIntosh Armory and Civil War
Museum
US Highway 441 and Avenue G
McIntosh, Florida 32664
(352) 591-2378

McIntosh Clock Repair
US Highway 441 and Avenue G
McIntosh, Florida 32664
(352) 591-2378

The Merrily Bed and Breakfast
Avenue G and 6th Street
McIntosh, Florida 32664
(352) 591-1180

O. Brisky's Book Barn
20656 US Highway 441
McIntosh, Florida 32664
(352) 591-2177

Rocky's Villa Restaurant
P. O. Box 806
1 mile south of McIntosh on
Highway 441
Orange Lake, Florida 32681
(352) 591-1809

Village Antiques
US Highway 441 and Avenue G
McIntosh, Florida 32664
(352) 591-2378

Events:
1890s Festival: third or fourth
weekend in October, (352) 591-
1180

INVERNESS

Alternative Gallery and Gifts/Carl
  Lundgren Art Studios
409 Courthouse Square
Inverness, Florida 34450
(352) 344-3460

Citrus County Chamber of
  Commerce
208 West Main Street
Inverness, Florida 34450
(352) 726-2801

Citrus County Historical Society
One Courthouse Square
Inverness, Florida 34450-4802
(352) 637-9925

The Crown Hotel
109 North Seminole Avenue
Inverness, Florida 34450
(352) 344-5555

Fort Cooper State Park
3100 South Old Floral City Road
(State Road 39)
Inverness, Florida 32650
(352) 726-0315

The Lake House Bed and Breakfast
8604 East Gospel Island Road
Inverness, Florida 34450
(352) 344-3586

Rails to Trails of the Withlacoochee
  Citizen's Support Organization
P. O. Box 807
Inverness, Florida 34451-0807
(352) 726-2251

Ritzy Rags and Glitzy Jewels
105B Courthouse Square
Inverness, Florida 34450
(352) 726-0024

Stumpknockers Restaurant
West Main Street
Inverness, Florida 34450
(352) 726-2212

Vanishing Breeds
105 West Main Street
Inverness, Florida 34450
(352) 726-0024

Wee Inverness Shop
105 Seminole Avenue
Inverness, Florida 34450
(352) 726-3114

Wild Bill's Airboat Tours
Route 44
Inverness, Florida 34450
(352) 726-6060

Withlacoochee State Trail
12549 State Park Boulevard
Clermont, Florida 34711
(352) 394-2280

Events:
  Festival of the Arts: first or second weekend in November,
  (352) 726-2801

FLORAL CITY, PINEOLA, ISTACHATTA,
AND NOBLETON

Antiques and Collectibles
7785 South Florida Avenue
(Highway 41)
Floral City, Florida 34436
(352) 344-4711

Carlotta's Antiques
8375 East Orange Avenue
Floral City, Florida 34436
(352) 344-3149

Lee's Coffee Shop
Highway 41
Floral City, Florida 34436
(352) 726-1378

Nobleton Boat Rental Outpost
Lake Lindsey Road
Nobleton, Florida 34661
(352) 796-7176
(800) 783-5284

Riverside Restaurant & Bar
29250 Lake Lindsey Road
Nobleton, Florida 34661
(352) 796-9669

Events:
  Strawberry Festival: first weekend
  in March, (352) 726-2801

  Heritage Days: (352) 637-9925

ARIPEKA, BAYPORT, AND OZELLO

Aripeka Fish Camp and Marina
Pasco County Road 595
Aripeka, Florida 34679

Aripeka Public Library
18834 Rosemary Road
Aripeka, Florida 34679

Peck's Old Port Cove Seafood
  Restaurant and Blue Crab Farm
West end of Ozello Trail
Ozello, Florida 34429
(352) 795-2806

Wench's Brew Food and Spirits
13982 Ozello Trail
(Ozello Trail at Waterman Road)
Ozello, Florida 34429
(352) 795-6900

Windflowers Studios
1129 South Ozello Trail
Crystal River/Ozello, Florida 34429
(352) 563-5416

WEBSTER AND TRILBY

E. C. Rowell Public Library/Civil
  War Museum
85 East Central Avenue
Webster, Florida 33597

Sumter County Farmer's Market
  and Flea Market
P. O. Box 62, Highway 471
Webster, Florida 33597
(352) 793-2021

Events:
  Annual Pepper Festival: third
  weekend in May, (352) 793-7541
  or (352) 793-2073

CHRISTMAS

Christmas Post Office
United States Postal Service
23580 East Colonial Drive (State
  Road 50)
Christmas, Florida 32709-9998
(407) 568-2941

Fort Christmas Historical Park
1300 Fort Christmas Road
Christmas, Florida 32709
(407) 568-4149

Fort Christmas Historical Society
(407) 568-4149

Events:
Fort Christmas Homecoming:
first weekend in October, (407)
568-4149

Cracker Christmas Festival: first
weekend in December, (407)
568-4149

DADE CITY

Azalea House Bed & Breakfast
37719 Meridian Avenue
Dade City, Florida 33523
(352) 523-1773

Church Street Antiques
14117 8th Street
Dade City, Florida 33525
(352) 523-2422

Edwinola Retirement Community
14235 Edwinola Way
Dade City, Florida 33525
(352) 567-6500

Glades Pottery and Gallery
37850 Meridian Avenue
Dade City, Florida 33525
(352) 523-0992

Greater Dade City Chamber of
Commerce
38035 Meridian Avenue
Dade City, Florida 33525
(352) 567-3769

Heart's Desire Antiques
14046 5th Street
Dade City, Florida 33525
(352) 523-1224

Lunch on Limoges
14139 7th Street
Dade City, Florida 33525
(352) 567-5685

The Osceola House
13941 7th Street
Dade City, Florida 33525
(352) 523-2008

The Picket Fence
37843 Meridian Avenue
Dade City, Florida 33525
(352) 523-1653

Pioneer Florida Museum
15602 Pioneer Museum Road
P. O. Box 335
Dade City, Florida 33526
(352) 567-0262

Sandbar Market
37832 Meridian Avenue
Dade City, Florida 33525
(352) 567-6818

Smith's Antiques and Gifts
37847 Meridian Avenue
Dade City, Florida 33525
(352) 567-5706

Tickle Your Fancy
37834 Meridian Avenue
Dade City, Florida 33525
(352) 567-3397

Events:
  Kumquat Festival: last weekend
  in January, (352) 567-3769

SOUTH REGION

CORTEZ

Annie's Bait and Tackle
4334 127th Street West
Cortez, Florida 34215
(941) 794-3580

Manatee Chamber of Commerce
P. O. Box 321
222 10th Street, West
Bradenton, Florida 34206
(941) 748-3411

N. E. Taylor Boatworks
c/o Alcee Taylor
P. O. Box 41
Cortez, Florida 34215

Nautical But Nice
12304 Cortez Road
Cortez, Florida 34215
(941) 795-5756

Events:
  Cortez Fishing Festival: third
  weekend in February, (941) 795-
  4637

ESTERO

Estero River Outfitters
20991 South Tamiami Trail
(Highway 41)
Estero, Florida 33928
(941) 992-4050
www.all-florida.com/swestero.htm

Koreshan State Historic Site
P. O. Box 7
Corkscrew Road and Highway 41
Estero, Florida 33928
(941) 992-0311

Koreshan Unity Foundation
P. O. Box 97
8661 Corkscrew Road
Estero, Florida 33928
(941) 992-2184

Events:
  Ghost Walk: full-moon weekends
  in January and February, (941)
  992-0311

  Archaeology Fair: last weekend in
  April, (941) 992-0311

  Olde Tyme Holiday Festival: second weekend in November,
  (941) 992-0311

STILTSVILLE

Biscayne National Park
P. O. Box 1270
Homestead, Florida 33090
(305) 247-PARK

Club Nautico Boat Rentals
2560 South Bayshore Drive
Coconut Grove, Florida
(305) 858-6258

Events:
  Fishing: every day

BIG PINE KEY

Bahia Honda State Park
36850 Overseas Highway
Big Pine Key, Florida 33043
(305) 872-2353

Barnacle Bed and Breakfast
1557 Long Beach Road
Big Pine Key, Florida 33043
(305) 872-3298
(800) 465-9100
http://cust.iamerica.net/barnacle

Lower Keys Chamber of Commerce
P.O. Box 430511
Mile Marker 31
Big Pine Key, Florida 33043-0511
(305) 872-2411
(800) 872-0752

National Key Deer Refuge
P. O. Box 430510
Big Pine Key, Florida 33043
(305) 872-2239

No Name Pub
North Watson Boulevard
Big Pine Key, Florida 33043
(305) 872-9115

Events:
   Underwater Music Festival: on
   the reefs at Looe Key, second
   weekend in July, (305) 872-2411

   Historic Seacraft Race (people-
   powered): first weekend in
   September, (305) 872-2411

   Island Art Festival: second weekend in December, (305) 872-
   2411

THREE BEACHES

MANASOTA KEY BEACH, FLAGLER BEACH, AND MEXICO BEACH

Driftwood Inn
2105 Highway 98
P. O. Box 13447
Mexico Beach, Florida 32410-3447
(850) 648-5126

Englewood Chamber of Commerce
(covers Manasota Key)
601 South Indiana Drive
Englewood, Florida 34223-3788
(941) 474-5511

Flagler Beach Chamber of
   Commerce
P. O. Box 5
Flagler Beach, Florida 32136-0005
(904) 439-0995

Lock and Key Restaurant
2045 North Beach Road
Manasota Key, Florida 34223
(941) 474-1517

Mexico Beach Chamber of
   Commerce
P. O. Box 13382
Mexico Beach, Florida 32410
(850) 648-5023

INDEX